PUT ME IN MY PLACE

PUT ME IN MY PLACE

DAVID W. HUGGETT

COVERDALE HOUSE PUBLISHERS
LONDON AND EASTBOURNE

ISBN 0 902088 58 0

Printed in Great Britain for Coverdale House Publishers Ltd.,
4a Balham Station Road, London SW12 9SG by
Hunt Barnard Printing Ltd., Aylesbury, Bucks.

Acknowledgements

A number of people have helped with their advice and information. I would particularly like to thank Mrs Janet Fraser of the Bible Churchmen's Missionary Society, and the Rev Gordon Jones, the Rector of Christ Church, Orpington, for their help. Also my gratitude is due to the College Principals, some of whom wrote most helpfully to me, and sent a great deal of information which space alone has prevented from being included. My thanks too to the Church Missionary Society for permission to include copies of their application forms. For some of the ideas in Chapter 9 I am indebted to the Rev Tom Houston of the British and Foreign Bible Society.

Contents

Contents

PART ONE
CALLED FOR SERVICE

What is a call?

He was young, intelligent and enthusiastic. His local Church listened sympathetically as he announced, 'I feel called to serve God in the ministry'. Naturally enough his fellow members were gratified to think that one of *their* young people should offer himself in this way. Perhaps a certain amount of merit accrued to the whole Church at this outstanding evidence of the spiritual success of their ministry.

So the ecclesiastical wheels were set in motion. The Church commended their young member to a suitable college, and then to the denominational powers that be. To each he said again, 'I feel called to serve God in the ministry'.

Four years hard study combined with practical service were followed by ordination and great rejoicing. Then a weary succession of failures. Our young hopeful passed on from one Church to another with as much regularity as some film stars change their partners – and with the same sort of growing disillusionment. Problems not only cropped up, but always seemed to get out of hand. They grew to crisis proportions. He moved on, and the sad story happened all over again.

Maybe you don't think that is a particularly unusual story. But here's the sting. Years of frustration and heartache later the minister of his home Church said to me, 'Of course we knew right at the start that he wasn't cut out for the ministry'.

Apart from the inevitable 'Why didn't they tell him?'

there are a number of other vital questions that the experience of that young man raises.

For instance, were they right, or was he? And how many people are there in full-time Christian service who have never been called? Or, to turn the coin over, now many people are there who are *not* in full-time Christian service, but who ought to be? Impossible to tell of course. No one has as yet carried out the kind of research that would be needed to tell us that. Yet a close look at the situation today reveals Christians in leadership positions who quite clearly ought not to be there, frequent losses from the ranks of full-time workers, and confusion among many as to what a call really is.

This must be regarded as a matter of great concern. The Church in Britain today is not strong enough, probably it never has been, to carry passengers or sustain such losses. On the other hand, if the challenges and opportunities of today are to be met effectively, then every single person equipped for leadership must be mobilised.

A great deal has been written and spoken about the need to involve the ordinary person in the pew. Undoubtedly that is necessary. At the same time leadership is vital People with the necessary gifts and calling need to be set aside by the Church to occupy key positions.

Another serious question must be raised. Perhaps after all that young man was right when he said, 'I feel called'. Maybe the trouble was that he misunderstood that call, or did not receive sufficient guidance from the Church in interpreting it so that he could find the area in which he could properly serve.

I grew up with a very narrow view of what a call is. All that I saw and heard indicated that you could be called only to the full-time home ministry, or to the overseas mission field. And that is still quite a wide interpretation of calling. Before our complicated twentieth century world demanded specialisation of one sort or another, such a broad classification may have been acceptable.

Nowadays vagueness like this will not do. If we are to

use our resources fully, and if we are to prevent square pegs getting into round holes, we must know as clearly as possible what God's call is, and to what specifically He is calling us.

Every Christian ought to give serious thought and prayer to the question 'Is God calling me to full-time Christian service?' It's not just an option for the extra keen or the super-spiritual. At the same time we need to be quite clear as to what such a call is, how its genuineness can be assessed, and how it can be obeyed.

But first an even more fundamental question needs to be raised: 'Is there such a thing as a call from God? Or is it simply a matter of each person deciding for himself what he will do?'

Clearly the Old Testament has many examples of men who received a specific call: Moses, David, Isaiah, to mention just a few.

The New Testament is equally clear. Initially we have the twelve Apostles. Their call is recorded in Mark 3:13ff. 'Afterwards he went up into the hills and summoned certain ones he chose, inviting them to come and join him there; and they did. Then he selected twelve of them to be his regular companions and to go out to preach and to cast out demons.'

Some of these men had already had a clear call in what might be described as direct confrontations with Jesus. The two sets of brothers, Peter and Andrew, and James and John had heard him say, 'Come along with me and I will show you how to fish for the souls of men' (Matt. 4:19). Levi had received a similar direct call, 'Come,' when he'd been engrossed in his paper work (Matt. 9:9). Nathaniel and Philip had also received a distinct, 'Come and see' command. As far as the other five apostles were concerned, apart from the occasion in Mark 3 already referred to, there is no record of a personal call, although that is not to say that they didn't have one.

At first sight the experience of these twelve men would seem to simplify the matter. Maybe we do not need to expect Christ to speak in a physical sense as he did by the

11

shores of the lake to Peter and his partners. But if someone is convinced that inwardly, in a spiritual sense, he has heard Jesus say, 'Come with me', that then is presumably evidence of a call. But is it? What then about the men who sincerely and earnestly say they feel called to the ministry, but who subsequently show a marked lack of aptitude for it? Can it be that God made a mistake? And what of the dozens who face the candidate committee of a missionary society and say with stars in their eyes, 'I feel called', only to return at the end of their first term of service (or before) to remain at home for good?

As for the rest of the New Testament there is again plenty of evidence that God called specific individuals into his service, but little in the way of a pattern by which that call came.

Paul, for instance, had a dramatic experience connected with the removal of his temporary blindness. In his later testimony in Jerusalem he clearly tells us that it was the words of a somewhat sceptical Christian in Antioch that constituted his call. 'You are to take his message everywhere, telling what you have seen and heard,' said Ananias (Acts 22:15).

Later, in Acts 13, Paul and Barnabas are called to missionary work by the Church in much the same way as Stephen had earlier been called to be a deacon. But when John Mark, Silas, and Timothy are called it appears to be a direct result of Paul's choice.

The point is that in none of these cases are we told clearly *how* God called them. We know that the Church chose Paul and Barnabas, and we know that it came as a result of fasting and praying but the actual mechanics of how they became convinced of the rightness of their decision is nowhere made clear.

The same could be said of Paul's choice of his colleagues, although he does say (1 Tim. 1:18) that there had been a prophecy received concerning Timothy.

A similar variety of experience is seen when we leave the

New Testament and look at the lives of well-known Christians.

The call came initially for Dr W. E. Sangster, the famous Methodist leader, when he was only fifteen. His Sunday School teacher, Robert Flenley, asked him when he left school, 'Have you ever thought of being a Methodist Minister?' Sangster said he hadn't. But that apparently harmless question was the seed, watered two years later by another friend asking almost precisely the same question, which later bore fruit in Sangster's application for ordination.

Nate Saint, the American missionary pilot, martyred with four of his fellow Americans in the Ecuador jungle in 1956, had a different experience. While on leave from the U.S. Army he heard the sixteen-year-old daughter of his host give a moving testimony. That set Nate thinking. Some days later a spiritual crisis came, and during a period of private prayer, to quote his own words, 'I saw things differently . . . BING . . . like that.' He knew now what he must do.

For Isobel Kuhn it was different again. In her book, *By Searching*, she tells us that her call to missionary work in China came through the reading of the book, *The Growth of a Soul*.

Another missionary received her call through a film. That was Helen Roseveare, well known for her courageous testimony during the time of the Congo uprising. While studying for a medical career she saw the film, *Three Miles High*, telling the story of the work of Major Leonard Moules in Tibet. Helen believed that the message of the film was for her, and she offered for overseas medical work.

Roy Orpin, a New Zealander, who was brutally murdered on his first tour of service in Thailand received his call through the singing of a hymn at an Easter camp.

On the other hand Hudson Taylor, who spent almost a life-time in China, simply received a clear inner conviction while praying that he must go to China.

A dramatic call, in keeping perhaps with his subsequent ministry as God's smuggler, came to Brother Andrew. He was in Amsterdam shortly after his conversion with his friend Kees. They decided to go to a large meeting being conducted by a well-known Dutch evangelist, Arne Donker. It was much like any other evangelistic meeting until almost the end of the sermon. Donker suddenly stopped and announced that he was sure there was someone there waiting to offer himself for missionary work. The announcement was followed by silence – embarrassing silence as far as Kees and Andrew were concerned. No one moved. Then Kees and Andrew got up to leave the meeting. And sat down again. At length they both gave in, and, responding to an inner urge which neither understood or approved, they walked to the front.

Just now the fact to note is that these individuals were unquestionably called for specific tasks. That there is no obvious stereotype indicates that we cannot expect a call to come to us in an identical fashion.

There seems to have been no doubt in the minds of these people that they were called by God. Nor, from subsequent events, does there seem any reason to question the rightness of their conviction. But what does interest us as a matter of vital importance is how they became convinced.

For instance it seems highly unlikely that Paul was convinced that he was to be the apostle to the Gentiles merely on the say so of a stranger who visited him in his lodgings in Damascus. He tells the Galatian Church of subsequent years of solitary preparation in Arabia before he began his life's work. During that time he would certainly have had plenty of opportunity to consider whether or not the call was genuine.

Very few people appear to have a sudden, dramatic call, without some period of heart-searching and decision-making. At a cursory glance, Acts 13 may appear to suggest that the sending out of Paul and Barnabas by the Church in Antioch was a simple matter: that it was all cut and dried. However, the mention of prayer and fasting makes it clear that there was a good deal of struggle on the part of the Christians, and probably on the part of Paul and Barnabas too, before the decision was made.

Go to a missionary meeting where new candidates for overseas are giving their testimonies before they leave. In the space of the few minutes that each will be given they cannot hope to do more than give a brief outline of the events that led them to offer for such work. They will be perfectly justified in using the kind of shorthand 'I felt called' phrase. You couldn't expect a long and detailed analysis of the thoughts, feelings, and struggles which led up to their decision. Perhaps some of them haven't even stopped to analyse them for their own benefit, much less yours.

They seem so sure. But how many of them will stay the course? And if they don't, will it be because, although they 'felt' called, in fact they weren't? Or because, although called, they misunderstood, and found themselves in the wrong place with the right motives?

Some will say that there is bound to be a certain amount of confusion and that it is impossible to lay down clear principles to prevent people from making these sorts of mistakes. 'There will always be wastages, they say. 'Human nature being what it is, mistakes are bound to occur.'

In which case the present chaotic situation must be part of God's pattern of things. Must it? Drop-outs. Wasted money and manpower. Disillusionment. Nervous and mental breakdowns. Years wasted in the wrong job. Square pegs in round holes. God is a God of order, not of such chaos.

In any case, men like Paul were sure. Why not you and me?

To be clear what we are wanting to be sure about we need to attempt some sort of definition of a 'call'.

There is first of all what we may describe as a *general* calling. In my own case I remember that my call began with the challenge of Mark 16:15. 'You are to go into all the world and preach the Good News to everyone, everywhere.' From there I needed to go on to discover just how God wanted me to fulfil the terms of that command. The point is that this first stage was only a very general call.

One in fact that every Christian has, whether or not he is prepared to recognise it.

That in itself was not sufficient to send me off to theological college or to a missionary training course, since it could well have been that I was to spread the good news in some other way.

Some zealous Christians enter upon a costly course of training with nothing more than a general call. They do not wait for an indication of how that general call is to be carried out specifically. The result is that they may spend three or four years reading theology – a noble and thoroughly worthwhile occupation of course – and at the end of it find that they have been equipped through an expensive training for work they will never do. A dubious stewardship of time and money to say the least.

If we suggest that the onus rests on the college to refuse people who have only a general call, we are not being realistic. They do refuse them of course, but colleges are largely dependent financially upon their students. In these days of high costs and relatively few applicants it is difficult for a college to justify turning down someone who is evidently enthusiastic and who claims to be called.

Things may have been different in the days when Campbell Morgan applied for the Methodist Ministry. He was in competition with no less than one hundred and fifty applicants. Only forty-five could be selected, and Morgan wasn't one of them. In that sort of situation it was comparatively easy to be choosey, and at the same time be guilty of refusing a man who was later to become an outstanding Christian leader.

The next important stage is what we may term *specific* calling. This is the inner conviction that God wants you to do a particular thing at this moment or at some time in the future.

Specific calling may refer to one's life's work. Paul's general calling was to preach the Gospel. His specific calling was to be the apostle to whom was entrusted the task of taking that Gospel to the Gentiles.

Within that responsibility Paul had further specific call-ings, as for instance when he heard the man from Macedonia saying, 'Come over here and help us' (Acts 16:9). But this in no way altered or modified the original specific call.

If we are going to commit ourselves to what may be a life of full-time service, then we will need a clear conviction that this is what God wants us to do. Not that He has to reveal the whole pattern to us in a cut and dried manner, but it does mean we must beware of a vague sort of general feel-ing. We need a deep conviction, supported by as much specific evidence as possible.

I was told by the minister to whom I first divulged my interest in the ministry, 'Don't go into it unless you have to'. He was undoubtedly thinking of the fact that every calling must be God-given. This was what made Paul so sure that he was 'under orders' to preach the Gospel. He didn't do it simply because he wanted to, but because he had a clearly defined objective to which God had called him.

A young Bible College student, Billy Graham by name, had the opportunity of talking with some of the great pre-war evangelists in America. Men like W. B. Riley bemoaned the fact that spiritual life in the States wasn't what it had once been. Or William Evans talked longingly of the great days of D. L. Moody. The result was that Billy had a growing burden for the spiritual state of his people. Here was the beginning of a call for him. But it was a general call. As yet no specific direction had been given. Had Billy gone forward on the basis of that burden alone he would have been ignoring the importance of God giving the specific call.

To put it another way. Every Christian needs a burden for the spiritual needs of those around – a general call. Not every Christian then receives a specific call to be a full-time evangelist. God could have directed Billy Graham in a number of ways. For him, first through the words of a friend, 'Billy, God has called you to preach,' and then through a lonely spiritual crisis, he was given God's specific call to evangelism.

Specific, God-given conviction that our service should

take a certain line is possible, provided that we are prepared to take time and trouble over it. That is what this book is designed to help you do.

The type of person God chooses

John Newton had a quite remarkable youth. Press-ganged into the Navy, a deserter, a slave in Africa, master of a slave trader, a Liverpool Customs officer, and finally an Anglican parson.

The deep inner struggle he had before deciding to adopt the latter calling was due to his awareness of the kind of life he had previously lived, which was so completely incompatible with his view of what an eighteenth century parson ought to be.

For us the problem is not so much his worthiness as his age. He was 33 when he came to accept the urgings of his friends to enter the ministry as a call from God. He was 39 before he began that work in Olney.

Now imagine yourself in a Church meeting or as a member of a committee set up to select a new minister. If you have ever been in such a situation you will recognise the following conversation.

'Now let's consider the man we had last Sunday,' says the Chairman. 'Mr Smithers he was called. Nice young fellow, don't you think?'

'Didn't think much of his sermon,' says a prim-looking business man.

'Well, I thought he was very nice,' says the elderly lady sitting next to him. 'He has a nice firm handshake, and his face – well it's sort of open. You know what I mean.'

'We mustn't get on to the colour of his eyes,' says the

Chairman and laughs loudly. Then more seriously he goes on, 'He's highly recommended.'

'By whom?' asks the prim businessman sharply.

'By his college principal.'

'Oh dear, so he's straight from college is he?' asks a permanently worried-looking man. 'It may be all right for some, but our Church needs someone with experience.'

'Yes, but we need someone who'll attract the young people,' says the elderly lady.

The worried man looks at her over his glasses. 'Some of us are not so young. We need someone with experience. Young, by all means, but with experience.'

Mr Smithers loses the vote.

Six weeks later the same selection committee meets. A certain Mr Norton is now being considered.

'Fine sermon . . . '

'Yes, one of the old school, don't you think?'

'He's certainly had experience . . . '

'Yes, five Churches in all. Must have learned something from them.'

'Wonder what he's like pastorally.'

'What's more to the point, what's he like with young people. He must be all of 55.'

'56 actually.'

'Oh my . . . !'

Silence, apart from the rustle of shaking heads.

Mr Norton loses the vote too.

When you begin to narrow it down you find that the ideal age for a full-time minister in this country is presumed to be somewhere between 35 and 40. Before that he's immature and the Church must train him. After that he's too old and the Church must endure him. Of course there are plenty of Churches that for one reason or another come into the category of the beggars rather than the choosers, so the pre-35s and the post-40s won't necessarily find themselves actually out of a job, although they may experience difficulty in getting one.

Colleges lay emphasis on youth. Although older students

are accepted, it is quite plain that the norm is the acceptance of students in their early 20s.

To be fair, there are great advantages in youth. Enthusiasm, for one thing, is often thought of as a youthful prerogative, although it would be quite wrong to suggest that someone over 40 can't be enthusiastic.

Certainly it is true to say that a young person will be less likely to be set in his ways. He would therefore tend to be more open to new ideas, and perhaps more likely to have them. He may also be readier to experiment. Mark you, a young man may also be less tolerant and tactful in the way he introduces new ways of doing things.

Again it's true that a young person may not be saddled with heavy commitments. The moment someone has a family and a house it becomes increasingly difficult to make the necessary adjustments to full-time service. Particularly is this true of overseas missionary work, where the society may not want to take on a whole family for purely economic reasons.

On the other hand, there are positive advantages in someone who is older. For instance, he will probably, although not certainly, be more mature. This will mean that he will have a far greater experience of life, and therefore be more likely to have an understanding of people.

He will also have had plenty of opportunity to have discovered his own strengths and weaknesses – and hopefully have done something about both.

He may lack some of the verve of a younger person, but at the same time if he becomes slower he may become surer also. He is then less likely to make blunders, immature decisions, or statements that cause offence.

God, we are told, is 'no respecter of persons', but we are. So we decide to pension a person off just when he may be reaching his point of greatest usefulness.

I know that there are problems of older people hanging on to jobs in the Christian Church which they have outgrown. Some don't know when it's time to make way for someone younger. They have to be told. But it is surely an incredible mistake to believe that a person necessarily reaches his peak around 35-40 and thereafter declines.

Perhaps we forget that Lloyd George became Prime Minister at the outset of the first world war when he was 53? Churchill was even older – 66 – when he began the most important period in his life. And de Gaulle was still going strong at over 80. Just to show that it isn't only politicians who may reach their prime relatively late in life, Lord Marks became chairman of Marks and Spencers when he was 60. These were men who, with a wealth of experience behind them, found their greatest usefulness just at the time when most are forcibly retired whether they are ready to be or not.

It is, I think you will agree, quite ridiculous to suggest that at the age of 64 years 11 months a man is capable of being a top-line executive, and one month later he is classed as useless.

This is not to criticise the use of young people in Christian service. God can use all the gifts and visions of youth. He will go on calling people in their teens and twenties to a lifetime of work. That should not rule out the fact that equally He can use older men and women, nor that some may not receive his call to service until the time when most are thinking of a cosy retirement.

If age is one area where we need to open our minds, sex is another. Constantly we hear missionary societies bemoaning the fact that they can't get enough men. They are very careful to say how much they need the women, but it is obvious that they would like a more even balance of the sexes.

What reason is there for this imbalance? Surely it can't be that God has miscalculated? Then why doesn't He do something about it? Or don't men respond in the same way? The home ministry, it's true, provides greater security and status for a family man whereas the prospect of periodic commuting between England and some overseas mission field for a lifetime may prove daunting when a wife and children have to be considered. A single woman is not subject to quite the same pressures.

Some have suggested, rather unkindly, that for many a single woman the missionary call is a kind of sublimation to compensate for her failure to get married. If that is so – and personally I doubt it in many cases – it does not explain why they should go overseas rather than serve in this country.

A much more likely reason is the comparative lack of opportunity for openings for women in full-time Christian work in this country. For many years the debate has been going on as to whether it is right to ordain women into the ministry. Apparently we have no qualms about sending them abroad, but we do about giving them the status of ordination in this country. Again we have no difficulty in allowing them to serve as a deaconess, or as a parish worker, but we do when it comes to the fully ordained ministry.

In fact most of the Free Churches recognise this anomaly, and have, in theory at least, announced their belief in the equality of the sexes in this, but fact has not yet caught up with theory. In 1971 the Baptist Union could only claim to have 16 women ministers out of a total of over 2,000 although, to be fair, that was a four-fold increase in four years. In the same year four per cent of the ministers accredited by the Congregational Union were women.

Go back to our ministerial selection committee for a moment. When the name of a woman minister is presented the members of the committee may state that they have nothing against a woman. But if then an equally suitable man's name is mentioned the chances are that the committee will quietly opt for the man.

Why this prejudice? Why do we gladly send women overseas, but give them little chance in this country? Michael Griffiths, in his book *Give up your Small Ambitions*, offers the opinion that the superior numbers of women in overseas missionary work is partly due to the larger number of women and children in the world for whom their talents are particularly acceptable. But if that is a valid point it would be equally natural to expect the same bias in favour of women ministers in Britain, for there is no denying the fact that women and children will be considerably more in evidence among those whom the minister will serve.

What is necessary is for the Christian individual and Churches to retain a perfectly open mind. That requires courage, for it may mean flying in the face of opposition. It also requires complete honesty both in dealing with Scripture, and in facing up to the realities of modern life.

It is a very long time since the name of Florence Nightingale passed into history as a constant reminder of the adequacy, and, in some respects, the superiority of women in certain spheres of life.

Mrs Barbara Enholc-Narzynska has been head of the Polish Bible Society since 1967, and although the only woman in such a position in the Bible Society world, she too shows the adequacy of a woman in Christian work.

Where pastoral responsibilities are concerned, a woman very often has gifts and a personality that makes her the superior of many men at present engaged in this work. In fact women are doing this sort of work, unpaid and unrecognised, as parsons' wives.

Besides age and sex there is another factor which in many minds prejudges the issue – education.

Since the general level of education has considerably increased, it is understandable that there should also be a desire on the part of the Church to raise the standards of its ministry.

No one, I imagine, would be foolish enough to suggest that education doesn't matter, or that we should discourage candidates for full-time work from reaching the highest possible academic attainments of which they are capable. At the same time education isn't everything – at least, education in the sense of formal examination successes.

After all, it is on record that both Napoleon and Churchill were near the bottom of their respective classes at school. It didn't stop them from becoming outstanding men. Nor need it stop you from becoming useful, even outstanding, in some form of Christian service.

In certain respects academic ability is a great advantage, but the very absence of it may be a greater spur to achievement. We've all known and envied the fellow scholar who shows promise of being brilliant. Sometimes later in life we've been surprised to discover that he has ended up very mediocre simply because he has always taken his ability for granted and never bothered to work at it. Whereas someone else, far less able, has made a great success of life simply because he'd plodded on doggedly, determined to overcome his lack.

Take Gladys Aylward as a shining example. It wasn't only the disadvantage of coming from a humble background, with, by the age of 26, only a parlour maid's experience. Worse than that she had shown in three month's hard study at the China Inland Mission Centre that she lacked the ability to pass the necessary examinations. After reciting her list of failures the Principal said kindly but firmly, 'Our experience tells us that after the age of thirty, unless pupils are quite exceptional, they find it extremely difficult to learn the Chinese language.'

Gladys was not exceptional. She was a failure. She knew that. She also knew with absolute clarity and conviction that she must go to China. So when the C.I.M. declined her application she refused to be daunted. And who today hasn't heard of the small woman who became such a dauntless missionary in spite of her early disadvantages?

There was of course no particular virtue in Gladys Aylward's lack of academic attainment, except that to a woman of her character it was a challenge that inspired her to all the greater effort.

Nor must we criticise the C.I.M. for turning her down and so robbing themselves of such an outstanding missionary. As far as they were concerned they could not afford to take that sort of risk.

The fact remains that in this country we have created a largely middle-class Church with a middle-class culture which therefore requires middle-class educational attainments on the part of its ministers. Theological and training colleges normally demand some sort of evidence of academic attainment as well as a sense of call.

Again we need the courage of open-mindedness. To Churches, colleges, missionary societies, I say, 'Don't expect candidates to conform to a set pattern, nor try to push students into a preconceived mould'.

And as for you, if you are reading this because you are interested in the subject of calling, don't close your mind. Don't assume that God can't or won't call you. Don't hide behind the fact that you think you're too old, or too young, or you're the wrong sex, or you haven't got the right G.C.E. passes.

The fact is – uncomfortable though it may be – God is still no respecter of persons. He calls Moses when he's 80, and Jeremiah when he's a young man. He calls women when we would have chosen men – and vice versa. He chooses great scholars like Paul and unlearned fishermen like Peter.

True, it's harder if you don't happen to fit the accepted pattern. If you're over 40 it won't be easy to find a mission board that will accept you. If you're a woman you won't find that Churches are exactly falling over each other to invite you to their ministry. And if you've never passed a single subject in G.C.E. the chances are that most colleges you apply to will tell you to go away and come back when you've rectified this.

There may be some perfectly good and several bad reasons for this. Those who tell you that you're too old, or the wrong sex, or too ignorant, are probably doing so to prevent you from disappointment because they know the general pattern of things. They are quite well aware of the difficulties that face the person who doesn't fit into the groove, and they are anxious to spare you them.

The fact is that God can, and sometimes does, turn upside down our preconceived ideas of what is usual and what is best. That He could call a man like Jacob with all his cunning and duplicity is an indication of what He can do with the most unpromising material. The all-important thing is to know beyond any shadow of doubt, with the stubborn single-mindedness of a Gladys Aylward, that God is calling you. If He is, then no difficulty is so great that it cannot be overcome, no drawback so serious that it cannot be the spur to great achievement.

That's why we must consider next how we can decide whether or not God is really calling us to serve Him in some particular, rather than just a general, kind of way.

Putting the call to the test

No one, however starry-eyed and idealistic, wants to decide on a course of action that may wrongly set the whole pattern of their life.

Two extremes have to be avoided. One is the super-spiritual attitude that considers it wrong to try to analyse one's possible call. A kind of inner constraint, however vaguely defined, is felt to be sufficient. The whole question of a 'call' is entirely subjective and largely described in terms of 'I feel called', or 'God wants me to . . . ' Such a calling dare not be questioned by the individual concerned, still less by his fellow Christians. An attitude like this may be adopted by the kind of person who makes for a strong natural leader, but who has little time for the opinions of others. Or it may be equally true of a sensitive and introspective person who does not relish others investigating the inner working of his heart any more than he enjoys a doctor poking about at his body.

At the other extreme we have the sort of person who likes to have everything buttoned up so neatly that there is no possibility at all of human error. If some divinely programmed computer could punch out a tape which clearly, and in great detail, spelled out the call, that would be fine.

Objective data is what is required, not only to avoid mistakes of human judgement, but also to excuse the individual from any lengthy period of wrestling with the problem. The fact that, as we have already seen, the call may come in widely differing ways makes it obvious that such a way of looking at it is quite out of the question.

Somewhere between the two lies the course to be steered. R. L. Child, writing in a booklet entitled *Concerning the Ministry*, published by the Baptist Union, says 'the constraint laid upon the heart and conscience, though deeply felt, may be hard to define'. That may be so. It does not prevent us from applying certain tests to that constraint to discover whether it is a genuine call of God or simply a thoroughly worthy, but general, desire to do something for Him.

First of all there are some negative points to be made. Eric Carlson, a Christian sociologist, makes the statement in the *Sociological Year Book of Religion in Britain* that 'much of the literature (on the subject of calling to the home ministry) is not so much vague as misleading'. He goes on to explain 'some . . . is misleading in that the ministry is elevated to the position of the only true form of discipleship . . . It is little short of spiritual extortion'.

You can see what he means. If some form of full-time Christian service is shown to be the superior thing for a Christian to do, there are one of two reactions you may have. You may decide that since you are a very ordinary Christian with no aspirations to grandeur, full-time work is therefore not for you. You'll settle for being a second-class Christian citizen. On the other hand you may decide that when you sang 'Just as I am . . . To be the best that I can be', you meant just that. And if that means becoming a minister or a missionary, then so be it.

This kind of heresy led in the Middle Ages to a 'double standard' of Christian conduct. The priests, nuns, monks, and hermits were expected to live at a higher spiritual level, and the peasant, shopkeeper, or the Lord of the Manor, however devout, however full of good works, just could not, and indeed were not expected to reach the same standards of spiritual living.

The same sort of double standard still lingers. 'Oh, but you're a minister', I've had said to me. The inference is that I'm expected to live in a different atmosphere. I shall not be subject to the same temptations. I have attained a status which other Christians might well envy because of its superiority.

Paul was in no doubt at all as to the privilege of being an apostle. But there were times when he indicated quite clearly that far from being the highest form of discipleship, it could be the lowest. He was a 'doulos' – bond-slave.

Arguing back and forward as to which is the highest form of service would be quite as futile as the Pharisaic arguments as to which was the first commandment. The all important question is whether or not *you* are called, and if so, to what. In order to get your thinking straight on that, put right out of your mind the idea that full-time service is the highest or the best. If you're called, then it's the highest and the best for *you*, but if you're not called then your highest and best is to be found in other service.

A mistake of a completely different order is to imagine that we must be called simply because people oppose us. Call it persecution complex if you like. It seems to be built in to most of us. 'When man condemns, God commends', is a perfectly true statement in certain circumstances but it is not an inflexible law.

When we think seriously about Christian calling, the chances are that we shall start hearing things, or interpreting what we hear in such a way that it becomes quite clear that the moment we announce our intention we shall be bitterly criticised and opposed. And this from those whose good opinion we hold very highly – parents, husband, wife, close friends.

We interpret this to mean that this will be just the first hurdle to overcome. After all it's perfectly true that some of those who have become outstanding servants of God have had to face this as the first real test of their call. It may be like that with you. On the other hand it may not. To know that there *will* be opposition of some sort is not a guarantee of a call.

The condemnation need not all be from the outside either. There is a kind of twisted reasoning which says, 'If I feel unworthy, it must mean that God wants me to do it'. But who wouldn't think himself unworthy if he takes the trouble to look objectively at all that a calling to full-time service will involve? It's perfectly true that if you are called and you feel worthy you'd better think again. But a feeling of unworthiness is not the same as a call.

A third mistake is to be attracted by the glamour of full-time work. That glamour still exists, there is no doubt. To be regarded as a 'real live missionary' or to be acclaimed for one's sermon can be very gratifying, and can give a romantic view to what is, particularly these days, a most difficult vocation. No one, however, is going to deny that being in the limelight hasn't got its advantages. For one thing it is very likely that your home Church and its minister will tend to put you on a rather special pedestal. Indeed, it's difficult not to do so.

The Church rightly regards it as a privilege to be able to send someone out from its ranks into full-time work. That person is therefore invited to the manse or vicarage, listened to with respect, looked up to, and generally placed in a pleasing position of prominence.

That's where the danger lies. All of us have a mental picture of what we would like to be – a kind of self-fulfilling dream. If that includes some idea of personal grandeur or importance mixed with a sincere desire to serve our Lord, we must be on our guard in case this of itself should be interpreted as a 'call'.

I'm not saying that an ambition to fill a full-time rôle in the Church is wrong. But to have a falsely romantic view of that rôle can mislead us into thinking that ambition and calling are the same thing. They are not. Paul says 'It is a true saying that if a man wants to be a church leader he has a good ambition' (1 Tim. 3:1). He then proceeds to demolish any romantic ideas of that leadership by outlining the responsibilities.

One last negative point must be made. The idea of the ministry or missionary work as a kind of retreat from inadequate personal testimony must be avoided like the plague.

I'm not much good at leading the conversation round to spiritual things. I don't find it easy to talk to others about my faith. I'm not a 'natural' as far as personal witnessing is concerned. But get me up in a pulpit and I can thunder away with the rest of them.

To some, being in full-time work is a kind of nailing of the colours to the mast. To be given a recognisable, albeit these days a not particularly high, status in society avoids the difficulty of having to try to explain to people who you are and what you stand for. They already know.

Such an attempted retreat from the difficulties and responsibilities of a personal witness is more apparent than real, as any full-time worker will tell you. In any case it is not sufficient to constitute a call.

But now let's try to be positive. How can I discover whether or not I am called to Christian service full time? It is well that we should take careful note of some of the mistaken ideas of what constitutes a call, but are there any serious tests I can make to discover whether those feelings I have, those thoughts, those dreams, those good intentions are really a call? Yes, there are.

Ask yourself first of all, *Do I want to do this work?* Leave aside for the moment the question of what particular form that service may take. We'll deal with that later. Whatever the work may be, do you *want* to do it?

When I use that word 'want' I use it in its strongest possible sense. I'm not talking about a vague sort of desire, as for instance you may have a bee in your bonnet about one day spending your holiday in the Canary Islands. I mean 'want' in the sense of a deep, passionate, insatiable desire. A desire that try as you will you can't get rid of. C. H. Spurgeon, when lecturing to his students, described it as 'an irresistible, overwhelming craving and raging thirst for telling to others what God has done to our own soul'.

If you haven't got that sort of desire, then you had better think again seriously. Any school teacher will tell you that there is a world of difference between the pupil who wants to learn and the one who doesn't. The latter won't get very far. Nor does the person who has taken up full-time work grudgingly. To do the job well demands that you want to do it and that you like doing it.

I remember a young candidate for work overseas saying to me that she was literally dreading going. She didn't want to do it. And there is a common misunderstanding that God only calls us to do something that we shall find distasteful. With a kind of spiritual masochism we offer to do the very thing we don't want to do simply because we think Jonah is typical of everyone who is called.

The same kind of error the mediaeval clerics to wear hair shirts, and made Bernard of Clairvaux sprinkle his food with ashes in the belief that God did not want him to enjoy the taste. What a sadly mistaken idea of God! I don't doubt that Jonah, up to a point, was an effective prophet. At least the people of Nineveh listened to what he had to say. But Jonah is given to us as an example of what to avoid rather than emulate. And there is no doubt in my mind that Bernard of Clairvaux would have written at least as beautiful hymns had he realised that God had given him 'all things to enjoy'.

So do you *want* to do this work? Is your ambition so great that you gladly say with Paul, 'I couldn't keep from preaching if I wanted to. I would be utterly miserable. Woe unto me if I don't' (1 Cor. 9:16). It may be – it should be – that you will feel totally inadequate. At times you may tremble at the idea of it. But running deep through all your conflicting emotions and changing moods there must be a strong desire to do this one thing with your life.

A second question we must ask ourselves – '*Is there any evidence that I am cut out to do this?*'

In a later chapter we shall be looking specifically at the

kind of gifts that are needed for full-time work, and how to discover what our gifts are. For the time being we can look at the matter in general terms.

The Church of Jesus Christ today suffers a great deal from sincere square pegs who are securely stuck in round holes. Sunday School teachers who can't teach, ministers of the Gospel who bore you to tears with their sermons, missionaries who quite frankly would have been far better off staying at home knitting woollen blanket squares for the 'wants' box – all these abound far too plentifully.

Maybe you think I overstate the case, or am being unnecessarily harsh. The point is that you should make sure that you do not add your name to the lengthy list of Christian misfits.

If you patently lack the necessary gifts, or if you have given no evidence as yet of your gifts bringing blessing to others, then it is too early for you to consider yourself called.

D. L. Moody did not become an outstanding evangelist simply because he thought it would be nice to do so. First, over a period of many months after his conversion, he invited young men off the street into the services of the Congregational Church in Chicago to which he belonged, and played a great part in leading many of them to Christ. Only after showing such evidence of an outstanding gift for soul-winning did he consider the possibility that God had a purpose for him as a full-time evangelist.

Of course I'm aware that it isn't always as neat or clearcut as that. Some people's gifts are not so immediately obvious. Maybe they need a good deal of drawing out before latent gifts can be developed. Or perhaps there are personal difficulties that have to be overcome first.

Robert Hall, for instance, became a fine Baptist preacher, yet during his first-ever sermon he broke down completely three times, while a missionary I know had to overcome a serious speech impediment before he could preach effectively. So don't imagine that you have to be a D. L. Moody or a Hudson Taylor overnight. It's more a question of latent gifts which you have discovered and begun to use and develop. Other gifts will develop as you go along that will confirm the course you have taken. But before you make any claims to calling be sure that there is some indication that you have the necessary gifts to fulfil it, for as John Newton says in one of his letters 'Surely, if the Lord sends a man to teach others, He will furnish him with the means'.

The third question we should put to ourselves is '*Do I have a deep conviction that I must do this work?*' If I haven't, then for the sake of my own spiritual life as well as for the sake of those I may minister to, I must keep out of full-time service.

That conviction has to be so deep that it cannot be shaken by any amount of opposition, sneering, apathy or cold-shouldering, whether it comes from friend or enemy.

Such conviction must be strong enough to remain steady through every kind of physical distress, discomfort, suffering.

It must also be able to see you through success and failure with equal certainty.

I'm not trying to suggest that opposition, suffering and failure are the only things you are likely to encounter in full-time Christian work. But encounter them you will, and unless you have an unshakable conviction that you are in the right place doing the right job, and that God has put you there, you will be in trouble.

That's why it isn't enough to be attracted by the apparent glamour of the ministry, or by your romantic notions of what a missionary is like. Nor is a simple concern over the great needs of the world sufficient unless you have at the same time a deep conviction that God is calling *you* to meet some of those needs in a particular way.

This is where so many have gone wrong. Because they want to help suffering mankind, because they have a deep compassion for people who are spiritually hungry, they feel that the desire to help on their part is the same as a call from God. It may be the beginning of a call. But it is not the same thing.

So look for a settled conviction in the matter. And if you

are in doubt about it, wait until the doubt is dispelled, and you know you have no other options.

That leads us to the fourth question. '*Am I prepared to wait and to put my call to the test of time?*'

The tendency, especially when one is young, is to think that there is a great need for haste. 'The king's business required haste' (1 Sam. 21:8) we quote as we listen to people who tell us with urgency of the millions who are dying without Christ. We are reminded too of the comparatively long time it has taken for the Gospel to spread so far, and therefore the relatively, maybe the extremely, short time there is left.

So the temptation is to be up and doing. That of course is quite right. There can, and indeed must, be a sense of urgency in our witness from the very moment of our conversion. But that has little or nothing to do with our call. Where that is concerned, God very often deals with us slowly and steadily. After all, it's going to affect the whole course of our life and, more sobering still, it's going to affect, for good or ill, the lives of a great many people. To make a mistake at this juncture can be a very costly thing.

One of the major advantages of the course of training normally demanded of those who enter full-time work is that it gives the individual three or four years during which he can literally fulfil the biblical injunctions to 'wait on the Lord'. Those are valuable years in which to put one's call to the test of time.

Naturally it is far better to do all one's waiting and testing before committing oneself to a lengthy and expensive course of training. Indeed most colleges will expect this of you, although there are a remarkable number of cases of individuals with just a few months' experience since their conversion entering a college, presumably with the intention of preparing for full-time work.

One last question. '*Is God opening up the way ahead?*'

Don't misunderstand this question. Because at first sight there are circumstances in front of you that are difficult, this does not necessarily mean that you shouldn't go ahead. If the Apostles had looked at the odds after the Ascension they would have concluded that they had better pack their bags and leave Jerusalem as quickly as possible. Instead they waited – and Pentecost happened.

But they did more than wait. They prayed. They were in fact, through prayer, looking for the way ahead. No indication is given us in the final words of Jesus to His disciples as to *how* the Holy Spirit was going to come on them and give them the power to carry out the incredible task that had been given them. God usually only shows the next step. So they prayed, and sought, and waited.

Later on in Acts 16 we find another instance of this kind of thing. Paul, Silas and Timothy were carrying out their God-given mission. They planned to preach in Bithynia but something stopped them. So they tried another way, and this time they received the go-ahead – 'Come over to Macedonia and help us'.

If you suspect that God may be calling you to full-time service take a long, hard look at your circumstances.

Take your family commitments, for instance. Have you responsibilities to a family? Would your offering for full-time service involve not just you, but them, in sacrifice; and if so, are they prepared for it?

Take your God-given physical and psychological make-up. Are there health problems, or personality weaknesses that would make you unfit for the stresses of full-time service? Are there any built-in physical drawbacks? For instance, if you have a quiet, thin, high-pitched voice, it's unlikely that you will make much of a preacher.

Take your experience. Has your commitment to a career denied you the experience in day-to-day Christian service and witness which forms an indispensable basis for full-time work?

Take your acceptance. Has your own Church, or a training college, or missionary society rejected you as unsuitable in some way?

We could go on. In point of fact, none of these is an

insuperable difficulty, but they must be taken into consideration as possible evidence of a mistaken call.

This does not mean that the moment some adverse circumstance comes you sit back, and with relief claim that God wasn't calling you after all. If that were the right attitude there would have been no famous Gladys Aylward. No. Set yourself to overcome the circumstance, or change it. At the same time, be alert. This may be God saying no.

Peter Marshall, who was later to become the Chaplain to the United States Senate, felt the call of God in 1924 when he was 22. Crossing the dark moors one night in Scotland, he heard his name called and, although at first he thought he was imagining things, it came a second time. He stopped dead in his tracks. Cautious investigation revealed that he was literally on the edge of a large stone quarry. Had the voice not stopped him he would have fallen to his death. Not unnaturally, such an amazing escape left Peter Marshall with the conviction that God had a special purpose for his life.

Later that year Peter Marshall heard a missionary speaking about China and the need for new missionaries there. Peter offered himself. But circumstances prevented it. With no father to provide the money, and no means of obtaining a scholarship for college, the door to China seemed fast shut. It was not until four years later, after emigration to the U.S.A., that Peter was able to begin training. By that time God had shown him that it wasn't to be China, but the United States.

A combination of waiting and reacting prayerfully to various circumstances had led Peter Marshall to where God wanted him to be.

36

The simple dynamics of decision making

If I had my way, God would make all the decisions That would be far simpler, and it would avoid all those mistakes I'm prone to make.

But that isn't the way it works out. If it did, I should be little more than a puppet on God's string. I would have no chance of going wrong, but at the same time I would have little opportunity of strengthening character and stretching faith. And if I am to occupy some position of trust and leadership within Christ's Church, then I am going to need both.

Even in the matter of calling, decision on our part is still necessary. This may surprise you, because you have read about Paul's compulsion to preach the Gospel, or the testimony of a servant of God like Gladys Aylward, you have assumed that the inner sense of conviction was so strong that it was inescapable. Once Paul had 'got the call' it was a simple enough matter of obedience. No further consideration on his part was necessary.

This is an over-simplification. It ignores the fact that, as we've already seen, the majority of people go through a period of heart-searching and spiritual struggle before they finally come to the point where they are convinced of a call. Even then they must decide whether that conviction is genuine, whether they are going to act upon it, and how they are going to implement it.

The making of a clear decision at this point is vital, if only because it will save following a costly course of action in entirely the wrong direction.

Maybe we have read with alarm of the comparatively large number of students who graduate from our universities and have great difficulty in obtaining a suitable job where they can use their training. Some, like the philosophy student who became a gardener, are drop-outs. Others happen to have chosen a profession that is already over-full. But many owe the situation to the fact that before they started their course they had no clear idea what they wanted to do at the end. They simply chose a course which interested them. Maybe because the more popular courses were already full, they studied an obscure subject like Arabic literature or military strategy, only to discover at the end of three years of fascinating work that a cruelly practical society had no use for their specialist knowledge.

That kind of costly mistake can only be avoided if the right decision is made at the outset. The Christian knows that it is also a question of good stewardship to make sure that the time, money, and effort that is invested in any course is directed to the right ends.

But when it comes to making even small decisions, many of us get all of a dither. Since we make dozens of minor decisions every day you'd think we'd have had sufficient practice when it comes to a major one. Unfortunately it isn't so. We either work ourselves into a state of emotional frustration because the more we think about it the more befuddled we become: or we allow events to take over and simply give up any pretence of making a decision. Subsequently we talk glibly about being 'led', when it would be nearer the truth to say that we drifted along entirely at the mercy of circumstances.

It is difficult to imagine that a man like Abram was guided in this way. Had he sat back and allowed events to decide his course of action, probably he would never have left Ur. A clear cut decision was needed, and evidently he knew how to make such a decision.

Naturally, prayer plays a large part in decision-making as far as the Christian is concerned. Indeed to try to make our decisions without prayer is to court disaster. At the same time, we are not thereby excused from the exercise of our reason – God given, and therefore of great importance.

'I'll pray about it', is the right and proper reaction when

38

we are faced with making a decision about our future. But if we think that there's an end of the matter, and that in some miraculous way we should hear a voice or see a sign that will make our way clear without further thought on our part, we are falling into the same error as those who forget that 'faith without works is dead'.

This chapter is not concerned with guidance as such, but only with one aspect of it – decision-making. If you want to know more about an admittedly intricate subject then you should read one of the books on it. (For my money I'd recommend *Guidance* by O. R. Barclay published by I.V.P.).

So how do we set about making the decision?

First get hold of all the facts you can. It is quite impossible to make a rational decision without all the facts. You can make a guess, or you can have a hunch. But it won't be a rational decision.

The sort of facts I mean are these: the different openings there are in Christian service, the gifts required, the types of training necessary, the cost of that training and what is involved in the actual service.

Some of these facts are fairly easily obtained, and this book is designed to supply as many as possible.

When it comes to the day-to-day facts about different types of service, it isn't so easy. If it is missionary work you are interested in you will do well to read as many missionary biographies, including modern ones, as you can. Also, get hold of missionary magazines and reports and any other literature you can. Build up as comprehensive a picture as possible of life as a missionary. And don't forget to read a book like *Who'd be a Missionary?* by Helen Morgan. It will help you to take off your rose-coloured spectacles and see missionary life as it really is.

Talk to as many 'real live' missionaries as you can persuade to listen and answer your questions. Dig deep. Interrogate them closely. Don't be put off by vague generalisations about the blessings or the satisfactions or for that matter the frustrations of their work. Nail them down to being specific. What is it really like? What things do they have to do that they like doing? And, just as important, what things do they have to do that they hate doing? And how about those things they are expected to do which they honestly feel are a waste of time? It isn't enough for you to know that sometimes they feel frustrated. Just exactly what are their problems? How about loneliness? Money? Marriage? Relationships with their fellow missionaries – especially their superiors? How much of their time is spent actually *being* a missionary, and how much is just a matter of keeping body and soul together?

The same sort of persistent questioning is equally important as far as any other kind of service is concerned. Don't be satisfied until you have all the facts. And try not to make your mind up one way or the other until you have a fairly comprehensive picture of the kind of thing to which you may be committing yourself.

Now you are in a position to take the next step – *analyse* the problem.

The analysis should take two directions. Begin by trying a little self-analysis. By this I mean asking the sort of questions that we touched on in the last chapter. Why do I want to do this? Have I got a clear picture of what it's all about, or am I blinding myself to things that I don't want to see? Does my picture of Christian service honestly match up to the facts? Or for that matter have I a rosy-coloured picture of myself, imagining that I can do a great deal which, if I'm honest with myself, I can't do? On the other hand have I too gloomy a picture of myself, excusing myself from service on the basis of my unworthiness?

Don't spend too long on this self-analysis, or like as not you'll end up with Elijah under the juniper tree! Particularly if you tend to be the quiet, introspective type, overdoing the self-analysis can become a kind of morbid self-indulgence.

Turn as quickly as possible to the analysis of the facts you have unearthed under step one above. At first you may feel that there is such a welter of facts – some of them apparently contradictory – that it is difficult for you to see your way through them. The more you turn them over in your mind the more confused you become.

So get them out of your mind and on to paper. Too simple to be sensible? Yet it is a very practical and helpful method of clarifying your thoughts. All you need is a piece of paper divided into two columns. In one of the columns you write down all the factors in favour of deciding to offer for a particular form of Christian service, and in the other all the factors against. Make sure that *every* point is listed.

Apart from the value of sifting through the pros and cons and so clarifying your mind, this method also has the advantage of putting in black and white, side by side, both the important factors and the irrelevant ones that are influencing you. If you are going to make a balanced decision, it is essential that you sort these out. Often, when set down in black and white, things which seemed so vital and loomed so large in our thinking are seen to be of minor significance, or maybe irrelevant altogether.

Take Moses as a first-class example of this method. Not that I'm suggesting he actually used paper and pencil, or wax tablet and stylus for that matter, but he did employ this technique: look at Exodus 4.

Moses is faced with a very difficult decision. Should he risk going back to Egypt? There he is wanted for questioning in connection with a murder. The job he's got to do there is the unlikely one of persuading the Pharoah to release a whole nation of valuable slaves on the very slim pretext that they want to worship God and they can't do it in Egypt.

Already you can see that the 'con' column is pretty formidable, and so far there's only one item in the 'pro' column – God has told him to do it.

But Moses isn't quite through filling up his 'con' column yet. He has three devastating factors to put there which must weigh down the scales heavily in favour of staying put as a shepherd. First there's the fact that nobody in Egypt is going to believe him, much less do what he tells them (v. 1). He either admits who he is and faces up to a murder charge, or he goes as a shepherd. Either way no one will believe his cock-and-bull story about meeting God in the desert. And as for the bush that caught fire . . . !

Moses puts another factor down in the 'con' column. He's no speaker. Not just a question of oratory either. He has a speech impediment. No one in his right senses would go in to a Pharoah, of all people, to try persuading him with that sort of handicap (v. 10).

And anyway there are plenty of other people who ought to go (v. 13). People who have greater gifts, and fewer handicaps. People who aren't murderers. People who are gifted speakers. People the Hebrews will listen to, and Pharoah too.

You can see that the evidence is pretty overwhelming, and sitting there mulling it over in the desert, these are the sort of things that would loom large with Moses.

But the 'pro' column isn't quite complete. Three factors Moses has overlooked. First (vv. 2-9) God promises to back up Moses with miracles. Second (vv. 11 and 12) since God makes mouths He is quite capable of dealing with the problem of a speech impediment. And third (vv. 14-17) He's going to send someone else, but that's no reason for Moses to opt out.

The average human mind finds it difficult to hold all the factors in balance at once. Like Moses we tend to look at one side of things – the side that happens to fit in best with what we want. And while we concentrate on one or two factors we blow them up out of all proportion.

Moses' 'cons' seem almost insuperable until they are put down in black and white alongside the 'pros'. Then it becomes immediately evident which side has all the weight.

Although here we are applying this method to deciding about 'calling' it is of course equally applicable to any decision that the Christian has to make. Get it down on paper in two columns, and it will surprise you how much clearer the whole problem becomes.

Don't be in a hurry over this stage. All of us tend to want to make our decisions overnight. We live in a world that gawks with admiration at the high-powered business man who has the ability to rattle off decisions with the rapidity of a machine gun. We don't always stop to ask how many of his decisions proved to be wrong, or had to be modified, or would have been improved had he taken a little longer in making them.

As far as calling is concerned there is little to be gained from making hasty decisions, and much to be gained from obeying the Biblical injunction to 'wait on the Lord'.

Once the decision is made, stick to it – for a while at least. No one wants to gain a reputation for chopping and changing. In any case it is only right to give your decision a chance. But despite all the precautions we take it is possible, simply because we are human, to make a wrong decision, and we have therefore to be willing to change it.

One thing we Christians are particularly bad at is admitting we are wrong. A lady of my acquaintance knew her husband was dying. The local Church prayed for him and was convinced that he would be healed. The lady was not. He died. Some in the Church accused the lady of lack of faith, and by implication this made her guilty of being an accessory to his death. Rather such cruelty than admit they had been wrong.

Not that it's easy to admit mistakes. And when you look back at any decision, right or wrong, you have made, you discover that God has overruled it. He has brought blessing from it. He has taught you lessons from it that you may not have learned in any other way. This is one of the marvellous things about God's care for His people. That should not, however, prevent us from honestly admitting when we have made a wrong decision, and making some attempt to put it right.

I may not have read widely enough, but in all the biographies of Christians I have read, I have yet to come across one in which wrong decisions are honestly stated. The assumption is made that the person was living so consistently close to God that he or she was always guided to do the right thing. But someone must have made a mistake when Gladys Aylward was turned down, or when Campbell

Morgan was refused for the ministry. And if in each case the committee made the mistake, it must be equally possible for there to be occasions when the individual makes mistakes.

Far better to have the courage to change a decision than to continue in a wrong course of action which will cause untold harm to the Church of Christ and create tensions within the individual which may well lead to illness.

Before we leave the subject of decision-making, there is a last point we must touch on briefly. And it's perhaps the most difficult of all to grasp because it seems to contradict some of the things that I've already been saying. Not that this need surprise us.

There's a great deal about Christ and His teaching that appears totally contradictory. It's this that gives the theologians such a tough time, because they tend to want things all sewn up neatly. Somehow Christian truth doesn't seem to lend itself to this.

Take for instance the great principle that Jesus laid down. 'Whoever loses his life for my sake will gain it' (Matt. 10 v. 39). Or again, 'The greatest one among you must be your servant' (Matt. 23:11). The whole matter of Christ's conquering death by dying, of overcoming evil by apparently submitting to it, is the supreme example of the outworking of this principle. And if you want to hear Him saying things that just about set everything we know to be true right upside down, then read again the beatitudes. Nothing more contrary to logic and experience than to say that the list of people He gives are the really happy ones.

When putting a possible call to the test and asking if it is genuine, we noted that one of the things we should be sure about is that we want to carry out a particular form of service. It's no use imagining that we shall make a good preacher if we detest preaching, or that we are cut out to be a missionary if we loathe the idea. Now for the contradiction. When we decide we have to be sure to notice that there is a strong element of sacrifice involved.

It is possible that the decision that is safe, sane, and sensible is the wrong one. The decision that looks like suicide, the end of a promising career, the opposite of common sense, and that causes our friends to doubt our sanity, may well be the right one. Nor is there any use trying to explain this logically, any more than you can explain how by losing your life you can find it, or how by dying Christ brought life.

But while we cannot explain it we can see it illustrated over and over again. In all the best fiction the hero comes to the crisis point in the story and decides that the only course of action open to him is to make some great personal sacrifice. As a result the problem of the story is solved, the hero is vindicated, or rewarded, and the reader goes away satisfied that because the hero made the right, though costly, decision, everything came right. And the unhappy ending story, which is not nearly so popular, is simply due to the hero making the safe and easy decision at the moment of crisis.

David Livingstone made the 'right' decision. We can safely say that with the hindsight of years. But at the time, what did it look like? A young Scottish doctor with excellent prospects of an outstanding medical career in front of him decides to throw it all up in order to become a missionary. He buries himself in an unknown continent far from the hospitals, the equipment, the books, the colleagues that could have combined to help him become one of the outstanding medical men of his time. No one can call that the safe, sane, sensible decision. Yet at the same time we know this was what he wanted to do. It was the right decision for him. Although we talk about it in terms of self-sacrifice, there was nothing else that would have satisfied him.

Don't opt for the safe, the easy, the secure, the un-costly. If you do, the result will be the unhappy ending story. And if I'm not much mistaken that is just the decision our affluent society has taken today.

The cost of serving

Inflation is, sadly, an 'in' word. But while we have come to regard it as an inevitable part of life, have we stopped to consider all its implications?

Some of those implications are spiritual. We all get caught up in it. Some out of greed, others out of necessity, find that material things take up a great deal of their thought and effort. Christians discover that they too are drawn into the overall materialistic climate. The result? Spiritual devaluation. As material (perhaps temporal would be a better word, for it's more than a question of money and possessions) things take up more and more of our attention, there is less and less room for the spiritual – a sort of spiritual devaluation.

Spiritual devaluation in its turn leads to a constantly rising cost in Christian service. And not simply in terms of a greater financial burden, although the yearly rise in Church and missionary societies' budgets shows this to be true too. There are all kinds of ways in which it costs more to be a Christian, simply because people are less interested in it.

Sooner or later we have to face up to the question 'What is my Christian service going to cost me?' And it's right that we should consider it carefully. To sing 'In full and glad surrender . . . Thine utterly, and only, and evermore to be', is fine but doesn't tell us, except in the broadest terms, what sacrifices are involved.

Mark you, sacrifice means different things to different people. Top dancers in companies like the Royal Ballet practise for 6 hours a day, on top of the hours of the performance. Their lives are strictly regimented. Many of the pastimes that others take for granted they are denied. We may perhaps describe these things as sacrifices, but they

46

tend not to regard them in that way because of their over-riding ambition to be top flight dancers. Other things take a place of lesser importance in view of the thing that consumes their attention.

I doubt if I need to apply that to the Christian Sacrifice is a very personal matter. Things that are a sacrifice for me may mean nothing at all to you because of a difference of temperament. We sometimes wrongly admire a missionary for the things that he has given up when he didn't care tuppence about those things anyway. A skylab astronaut is reported by his wife not to care at all that he gets no more pay for his dangerous mission than the regular U.S. Navy captain, because it's the job that matters to him, not the money. To someone for whom the money *did* matter it would be a sacrifice to become an astronaut.

Sorry if I'm labouring this point but it is important to get things in perspective. As we noted in the last chapter there are some aspects of Christianity that appear quite contradictory – the way of blessing is through sacrifice, for instance. But we must be clear what we mean when we talk about sacrifice.

So when I list some of the more obvious sacrifices we shall have to make, you may have to add some of your own, and at the same time cancel out some that aren't important as far as you are concerned.

1. Security

No one who is reading this book is, I'm quite sure, under the illusion that a fortune is to be made out of Christian service. There was a time once in England when to go 'into the Church' was a career. The parson was a professional man of some standing, and often of some wealth too. But inflation has left him far behind.

In a recent inquiry in a northern town it was discovered that in the ten years since 1963 many teachers' salaries had risen by more than three times, while the Baptist minister's had just doubled. And teachers are badly paid.

The situation differs according to the denomination or the

missionary society in which one serves. The more wealthy manage to maintain their workers at a reasonable standard of living, while the less fortunate find themselves below the poverty line, and dependent upon the state to eke out a living.

At this point we are not concerned to ask why this is so, or to suggest remedies, but simply to make a statement of fact. It is a matter of sacrifice to be taken into consideration.

And before you dismiss it in the first flush of enthusiasm, telling yourself that money has never bothered you, try imagining it in a few years' time. A wife in tears because she can't make ends meet for the visitors coming on Sunday. Your child growing bitter because at school they laugh at her in shabby hand-me-down clothes. Your own feelings when you discover the large number of your Church members who pay more in tax than you earn in a year. All comparatively small matters, but as Elijah found under the juniper tree, it's very often the small, niggling things that can get out of all proportion when you are weary, or depressed, or just plain out of sorts.

Perhaps one of the greatest single causes for a sense of insecurity is the problem of retirement. In chapter 2 we noted that an arbitrary retirement age is a problem in itself. But at present it's a fact, and very little preparation is made for it. Unless a full-time Christian worker has rich relatives who can leave him a tidy sum of money, when he comes to the age when most other people can sit back and enjoy the well-earned fruits of a life-time of work, he has to start worrying about finding a house and making his pittance of a pension buy it as well as keep him, or else hopefully rely on the charity of others.

In case you should think that I'm painting the picture blacker than it is, ask any retired minister or missionary. But they probably won't admit it, because they are mostly that rare kind of person who regards such sacrifice as a small price to pay for the privilege of a life of service for Christ.

Or in case you think that it's unspiritual to put these things

48

down in black and white, remember that Jesus said himself, 'don't begin until you count the cost. For who would begin construction of a building without first getting estimates and then checking to see if he has enough money to pay the bills?' (Luke 14:28).

Not that insecurity is all bad. Shakespeare said 'Security is mortals' chiefest enemy' (Macbeth). Or to quote a modern scriptwriter, Terry Nation, 'Security is the most destructive thing in modern life, especially to creativity'. Of course it's true. A sense of security can sometimes undermine our trust in God. Just as long as you know the score!

2. Status

The New Testament never promises us status. That's quite plain. But in a subtle way this too has become part of the increased price of modern spiritual devaluation.

Once the 'clergy' were respected professional men, and the white missionary was a cut far above the humble native. Now, although still technically counted as part of the professional class simply because of its vocational emphasis, the Christian worker no longer is given that general respect that once put him in a position of some influence in the community, ensuring a hearing for his message.

With the growth of secularism the professional Christian has become rather the object of people's pity. He is an anachronism whose preaching is largely irrelevant, and whose pastoral work has been taken over by the state. With typical British tolerance we do not actually want to get rid of him, but we are at a loss to know what to do with him. With his curious clerical garb and in some cases elaborate vestments, he seems little more than part of the tourist attraction his Church has so often become.

Even within the Church his status has fallen. The modern emphasis upon the importance of the layman has led to many full-time workers feeling threatened.

Overseas, too, the men and women who were once given pride of place because they were white missionaries now find themselves in subordinate positions, and that by invitation of the national Church.

Maybe this isn't such a bad thing. The picture of a professional man with a social status isn't all that close to the New Testament portrait of Christ or his followers. But since this is how it has developed you had better be aware of it, and if status – being somebody – means anything to you, then you should be aware that there's a price to be paid here too.

3. Family

Henry Martyn, ready to embark for his life's work in India, fell in love with a charming young lady, Lydia Grenfell. The curious social restraints of 1805 meant that they had very little time together to get to know one another, and Henry left his proposal of marriage until he was actually leaving. Hardly surprising then that Lydia found it impossible to accept at such short notice, and Henry was forced to leave England a single man. And he remained so. Maybe it was for the best. Undoubtedly the rigours of missionary life in India at that time would have made great demands upon any woman.

To imagine something like that happening today is difficult. None of those social restraints apply. Reducing inhibitions has at least made it possible to give time to considering what faces anyone about to undertake Christian service.

Just now I'm not concerned with the question of whether it is right for you to marry or not. What *is* right is to count the cost, and if you are courting or engaged to count it together.

In some ways it's simpler if you're planning on missionary service abroad, because the decisions are clear cut. The fact that you must cut ties so completely and start out on a totally different life makes it essential that you should both be totally committed – not just to each other, but to the work as well.

At home it's different. For instance, some ministers' wives

do not have their hearts in their husband's work. Desperately they want to be just an ordinary wife. They want an ordinary husband who will get on with his profession like any other husband. And it just can't be done. Where Christian work is concerned both are involved – and the children as well. The sacrifices that have to be made have to be shared by the whole family. So count that cost too. And before you make a glib consecration remember that you are to some extent involving wife and children.

I believe this was why Paul appears to have a down on marriage. Not because he was against it, nor because he felt that the Christian worker had no right to it. But he knew that for someone like himself, with such a consuming passion – a mania we could call it – the strains imposed upon a marriage would be virtually intolerable, and certainly unfair on any normal woman.

I've known a vicar whose children accused him 'Daddy, you're married to the Church', another Christian worker whose children announced 'We want a father', and numerous wives who have suffered a silent loneliness because their husbands were 'burning themselves out for the Lord'. If you want to be that type of worker, then probably Paul's words are for you. Better not marry than sacrifice a wife and family on the altar of your own consecration.

4· Work

You don't need me to tell you that Christian service is hard work – I hope! 'What *do* you do with your time?' one church member asked me, obviously influenced by one of the many quips about parsons working one day in seven. But for the Christian worker there's no such thing as the thirty or even the forty hour week. It's much more likely to be around 60. Even those times when you're not working you will be on call.

Foster-Harris of the University of Oklahoma's creative writing unit says that writing is such a demanding occupation that even the professional writer can normally only put in about 4 hours a day. The Christian worker soon finds that

51

the same is true of preparing sermons, Bible studies, and the like.

On top of these he has the demanding tasks of visitation and spiritual counselling. There are the interminable meetings and committees he is expected to attend. A considerable amount of routine correspondence and other administrative detail to attend to. If he's a missionary he'll have to add language study, the cultivation of his vegetables, and a host of other daily jobs. The laugh of it is that many people fondly imagine that he or she has been set aside from the normal busy life to enjoy quiet, prayer and meditation which will in turn lead to deep and soul-satisfying sermons and inspiring leadership.

As a Church we often impose intolerable burdens upon the servants of Christ, and when Sunday comes we complain with Milton that 'the hungry sheep look up and are not fed'. A great deal of re-thinking needs to be done in this direction.

5. Pride

Just one more thing that needs to be high-lighted – pride. But not pride in its more general aspects. I mean pride in a particular sense.

We all know that it is 'more blessed to give than to receive'. Did you know that it is also a good deal easier? True, there are some people who are born scroungers, looking upon it as their natural right to get whatever they can from others. But anyone with any self-respect, or pride – there's the word – will hate receiving charity.

Yet if you are not prepared to swallow your pride – and swallow pretty hard at times – when the cheques come at Christmas, or the clothes, or the bags of fruit from the harvest festival, you will not only be the poorer yourself, but also you will create a good deal of ill-feeling.

I know a missionary who once received a parcel of cast-off clothing as a gift. When he and his wife opened it they found that it hadn't even been washed – not even the underwear. It takes some humility to accept that sort of charity cheerfully and graciously. Fortunately it doesn't happen often.

Well, sit down and count the cost. By all means do it carefully and fully. But when it's all done, remember Jesus became poor for our sakes. Never look at your personal sacrifices, whatever they may be, without reference to Him.

The role of the Church

So far we have been thinking of the Christian's vocation as a very personal thing. To emphasise the individual's liberty and responsibility to God's call is essential. No one has the right to dictate to another what he must do.

At the same time it is wrong to assume that we have the right to go off and just 'do our own thing', as if the Church did not exist and we were not members of it.

In 1785 William Carey, who was in the opinion of many to become the founder of modern Christian missions, applied to the Baptist Church at Olney for membership and also for their approval that he should be set aside for the ministry. That in itself shows Carey's awareness of the need to receive the blessing of the local Church before he took up pastoral service. Today, at least if one hopes to serve one of the main denominations or missionary societies, it is still necessary to get the backing of one's home Church.

But a closer study of Carey's application reveals the interesting fact that he had previously been approached by other Churches before he had ever thought of offering himself for the ministry. For instance, in 1779, shortly after his conversion he was 'pressed into taking public part in the Sabbath evening conferences'. Three years later he accepted an invitation to preach on a regular fortnightly basis at

Earls Barton. And when in 1885 he requested the Olney Church to approve his call to the ministry, it was only because he had already received invitations from both Earls Barton and Moulton to become pastor.

In other words, Carey did not offer himself for the ministry until first he had been convinced by the approaches of the Church that it was right to do so. This doesn't mean that he had no inner sense of a call, or that he was simply a conscript being unwillingly drafted into the army of God's full-time servants. Far from it. But it does mean that the Church, rather than Carey, took the initiative.

This seems in line with the teaching and experience of the New Testament. Already in Chapter 1 we have referred to the main passages in the New Testament which clearly show that the Church selected and sent out missionaries. 'Brothers, choose seven men among you who are known to be full of the Holy Spirit and wisdom . . . ' (Acts 6:3), and ' . . . the Holy Spirit said to them "Set apart for me Barnabas and Saul, to do the work to which I have called them" ' (Acts 13:2) are passages which indicate the two-sided nature of Christian calling.

The Church then has the twofold function of selecting Christian workers, and also of confirming or rejecting those who offer themselves. But how can it carry out that function?

First of all the Church – and that means the sum total of the membership, although in the nature of things the leaders will be particularly involved – needs to have a close and intimate knowledge of its members. It should be quite obvious that you cannot select potential full-time workers unless you know the material you are working with.

At present, it seems to me, the situation is a thoroughly unsatisfactory one. Although the word fellowship is bandied about freely as if everybody knew exactly what it involved, in fact few of us have a deep practical experience of all its implications. We know far too little about each other, and far too little is done to see that an individual's gifts are discovered and matched to the needs of the Church as a whole.

If the Church is to be on the look-out for possible full-time Christian workers, it must be aware of the gifts present within the fellowship as well as the spiritual calibre of its members.

The same is true in relation to the Church's role of confirming the call of someone who offers. Frequently the Church is given no opportunity to comment on a person who has announced their call to full-time work. Presumably it is felt to be an impertinence. Or perhaps it is regarded as the duty of a college or distant committee. But it is the home Church that should know the candidate in some depth.

In fact this should be part of the Church's normal work, and not simply related to candidates for full-time service. Instead we find more often than not Churches desperately appealing for people to serve in the Sunday School or the youth club, or whatever else it may be, and then being in the position of virtually having to accept anyone who offers. The suitability of the person is secondary. Willingness is primary.

The maximum use of manpower depends upon the right person doing the job he or she is fitted for. This involves the Church in being aware of what gifts are already being used, and also what potential gifts are available.

I suspect that many a Parochial Church Council or Church Meeting faced with such a responsibility would visibly wilt, simply because for too long we have left it entirely to the individual. Making time on busy agendas for more than the routine items of Church fabric and finance is no easy matter. Yet it must be done.

In the case of John Bunyan it was a number of the spiritually-minded members of the congregation in Bedford who approached him and urged him to begin to preach. Interestingly, we are told that Bunyan 'was dismayed'. But he eventually agreed to their request and began accompanying other preachers in and around Bedford, adding a brief word of his own. It was not long before his preaching gift was being exercised with considerable effect.

In his case the Church saw his potential gifts, gave opportunities for their exercise and development, and finally gave them the stamp of their official approval. Were this done more frequently today there would be fewer preachers in our pulpits who cannot preach, fewer pastors who cannot shepherd, fewer administrators who are born muddlers.

However, all this may not seem to be of much immediate practical use to you if you are considering the possibility of your being called by God. Unless you happen to be a fortunate member of one of those few Churches that do make an attempt to do what I have outlined above, you may have to content yourself with deciding that, if you are ever in a position of leadership yourself, you will see to it that the Church you lead takes its responsibilities seriously, and is trained to look for gifts and encourage their use. For the present you may have to make the best of a bad job.

The fact that many Churches do not fulfil their rôle of choosing out potential Christian workers and preparing them for service does not mean that you can ignore the Church. With all its imperfections it is still the body of Christ. Therefore, as soon as possible, you should share your own growing conviction of a call. A candidates' secretary for a missionary society told me that many students seem to regard their home Church as the last people to be told of their intentions. That ought not to be so.

Ideally one ought also to be able to expect the Church to give guidance about the needs and opportunities of Christian service, and the varieties available. Generally speaking, most Churches select a short list of missionary societies to support. Sometimes the choice is limited to a denominational society, or to those in which members of that particular Church are serving. The reason for this is obvious. Prayer support and giving will be spread very thin if too many societies are invited to plead their cause. The unfortunate result, however, is that the Church's understanding is strictly limited, and knowledge useful to the intending full-time worker is scanty. Instead of an overall picture of up-to-date needs and trends, both in this country and overseas, the inquirer is left with the impossible task of deciding just where to start in assessing the situation.

Such a black picture is happily not true of every Church. Most however, are just not geared to providing this initial information, or even have any idea where to turn to find the facts that are needed.

Obviously a massive effort in Christian education is needed. First of all the needs of the Church at large must be regarded as of primary concern to the local Church. To plead that we are too busy looking after our own local work to be concerned in any one else's is totally inadequate.

Secondly someone (or even better, more than one person) in the Church needs to be given the specific task of collecting information and of making the Church aware of the sources of further information. The membership will then be in a position to start an intelligent assessment of each other's gifts, and the matching of those gifts to the needs of the Church.

This is not the end of the process, of course. Detailed information can only be expected from those intimately involved in various forms of the Church's work. That need not be the local Church's job.

Incidentally there is sometimes the tendency to avoid consulting the minister, vicar, or elders. Maybe in the first flush of enthusiasm, the local Church leaders appear to you to be lacking in zeal. Or perhaps the intimacy of a call from God makes it easier for you to approach someone you know less well – someone who will not show surprise at your being chosen.

Yet the chances are that if you do make the approach, not only will you discover that the vicar, or minister, or whoever leads your local Church is a good deal more enthusiastic than at first you supposed, but also he is much wiser and more knowledgeable. Simple courtesy demands your approach to him, in any event, and in most cases he will be anxious to give you the help and advice you need.

PART TWO
OPPORTUNITIES FOR SERVICE

Different levels of ministry

Traditionally there has never appeared to be any difficulty in defining what we mean by 'full-time' Christian service. The Church from quite early on has been neatly divided into the clergy and the laity. No one ever seemed to doubt that this was how it should be. The only dissension to ruffle the complacent was the frequent debate about the ranks within the full-time ministry – the meaning of the words bishop, presbyter, priest, deacon.

As to defining what was meant by full-time service, why bother? The name was self-explanatory. It simply meant that the person concerned was giving his whole time to this work. He had no other job. A secondary, but important, additional factor followed – he was entirely dependent upon his Christian service for his income.

Even when some objected to what they called 'the one-man ministry', they still felt it necessary to set aside some, particularly for overseas work, in a full-time capacity.

Then came the objection to the 'full-time service' on the grounds that it is thoroughly misleading. All Christian service is full-time – or should be. If it isn't, then there is something wrong with your Christianity. You can't treat Christian service as if it were simply a hobby. A Christian is a Christian 24 hours every day.

Nowadays the edges are becoming more blurred. Overseas many countries refuse western missionaries unless they are professionally equipped as teachers, doctors, nurses, agriculturalists and so on. Some are even supported by the government and give their Christian service part-time. Even many of those who are wholly supported by a missionary society would admit that their specific Christian activity is to some extent limited to the silent witness of life while carrying on their profession.

On the other hand, one man I know went out to Africa as an employee of a bank to serve Christ part-time. He has been instrumental in leading many to Christ and establishing new Churches, although he is not on any missionary society's pay roll. Who is to say that he is any less of a missionary?

In Britain the picture is similar. Even among those who are still regarded as being in full-time service there are many who are forced by simple economics to take on some part time job, or allow their wives to go out to work in order to make ends meet.

The difficulty is to find a suitable alternative title that will cover all the forms of service that demand what we called in Chapter 1 a specific rather than a general call. If we regard it all as simply 'Christian service', where do we draw the line between various forms? Aren't we back to the problem of distinguishing between the 2 types of calling? On the other hand, if we call it 'special' Christian service, or a name like that, aren't we in danger of setting it up as something better, and the people who engage in it as a cut above their fellow Christians?

In my view the breaking down of the old division between 'full-time' and every other kind of service is a necessary part of the Church's rediscovery of what the New Testament calls the priesthood of all members of the Church. Put quite simply, this means that every Christian has an active and vital part to play in the functioning of the Church. No one has the right to sit back passively simply because certain so called 'full-time' professionals have been appointed to do the work for them.

At the same time, it is evident that there has always been a need for those who, by reason of their gifts, experience, and training, are to exercise specialised functions in the Church.

Those two words, *specialised functions*, I am going to adopt as an alternative to full-time service. They may not be ideal. Perhaps you can come up with something better. I choose them because a *specialist*, so my dictionary tells me, is a person set apart for a particular duty, and because *function* puts the emphasis where it belongs – upon the duty being done, and not upon the rank, fancied or otherwise, of the person who is doing it.

Such ministry has no necessary connection with the amount of time spent on it each day, nor with the question of income.

Yet we are not quite finished with the term 'full-time', because obviously this may be applied to *specialised functions*. What are the advantages of anyone giving their whole time to and depending entirely for their income on specialised functions?

There are some obvious advantages. For one thing, such a person is more readily available. Particularly in those functions which deal largely with people this is important. Imagine the following conversation –

'Excuse me, Paul . . . '

'Look Priscilla, how many times have I told you not to interrupt me when I'm busy. And you didn't knock . . . '

'I'm sorry, but there's this fellow outside.'

'I'm far too busy. I can't be bothered today. Anyway I've got this order for tents. It must be finished for tomorrow.'

'But he says he must see you. He wants to know more about the Christian way.'

'Oh bother! Very well, I suppose I'd better see him, but I hope he doesn't keep me too long.'

Ludicrous isn't it? On the other hand, not too much should be made of availability. Even the minister must have his day off and the missionary his furlough.

Another obvious advantage is that there is much greater opportunity to spend time in prayer and study – *both* of which are vital to really effective service. The business man who rushes home at the end of a hectic day, is held up because his train is running late and finally, in between household chores, the clamour of the children and the telephone, manages to spend a few stolen moments preparing his Sunday school lesson for next week, envies the man who has all day in which to follow his Christian calling.

Only it doesn't work out anywhere near that simply. The man who has plenty of time for prayer and study can quickly become harassed by those who believe he has nothing better to do all day than attend to their needs. As for the welter of humdrum details and routine ecclesiastical chores, they soon threaten to drown him. Stern self-discipline and an iron will are required to make sure that the advantage of increased time is not frittered away.

As for the disadvantages, well, there are those too. Apart from the multitude of petty things that can side-track one from the main purpose of one's specialised function, it is also possible to become so engrossed in legitimate and necessary Christian activities that one becomes isolated from the world, and therefore unable to communicate with it. The very nature of a calling to a specialised and particular job tends, if one is not very careful, to foster an 'ivory tower' kind of mentality. Particularly is this so if we are in it full time. Members of any profession are apt to be in a small world of their own. They talk an 'in' language, and look for their friends among those with similar interests. But when a servant of Christ becomes a professional in this sense he is in danger of becoming totally useless as a witness to his faith.

A disadvantage of a different kind is the financial drain on the resources of the Church made by full-time specialised functions. For instance it is not unusual for more than half a Church's income to be spent paying the minister. When lighting, heating, repairs, and the many other expenses of running a Church are added to this, there is precious little left for supporting overseas missions, or for providing necessary equipment and literature for local evangelism.

Often the unfortunate result is that the Church regards its

commitment to its full-time staff as its primary, if not total, expression of mission in the locality. Then we are back with the situation of a professional clergy expected to do the work that really belongs to the Church, and the double standard which sets the full-time worker as a cut above the rest of the membership.

Nor can we avoid the fact that for years now, alongside the rapid inflation which affects churches and missionary societies as much as everyone else, there has been a steady decline in church membership. When increased costs are met by diminishing resources, it needs no prophet to anticipate the resulting financial strain.

Some strongly believe that the steady trickle of people in recent years who have exchanged full-time status for part-time is God's way of answering the situation. This is not to say that there is now no place for full-time workers. They will always be greatly needed. The long-term solution lies in reversing the downward trend in church statistics. But financial stringency may perhaps be one of God's methods of forcing us to look again at what we have called specialised functions, and to realise that 'full time' is not the only way of exercising them.

Naturally, when we turn to consider part-time work, some of its advantages are the opposite of those disadvantages of full-time service we have just been considering.

Take finance. If a part, or maybe even most, of one's income derives from a job other than Christian work, the financial load on the Church is considerably reduced.

For the part-timer, too, there is little chance of that 'ivory tower' mentality. With one's feet by the work bench, or behind the bank counter, or in the staff room it is much easier to remain in firm contact with ordinary people. To be faced with the same problems of making ends meet, paying the mortgage, commuting to work, all helps to make people feel that you are approachable.

But there are disadvantages too. Sometimes churches that are quite happy to have part-time leadership rather than none at all regard that leadership as of inferior quality. This,

I suppose, has something to do with the rosy-coloured, almost magical aura, with which we still surround certain types of ministry.

Alongside this attitude there often goes the expectation that the part-timer will be able to do just as much work as a full-timer, mainly because many people still find it quite impossible to believe that the latter can really find enough significant things to do to fill up his time.

Then another disadvantage – the difficulty of holding down two jobs effectively. And perhaps an even greater problem – that of finding a suitable second job which will allow sufficient time and energy to be left over for the demanding spiritual work of Christian service.

Already there are far too many Christian people who suffer from mental and nervous exhaustion. In many cases it is simply that they have allowed themselves to become over-committed.

Ideally the second job you undertake should not be too taxing. It should not carry heavy responsibilities. It should not have long hours. Ideally, too, it should be as strong a contrast as possible to the Christian work in which you're involved.

Unfortunately the ideal is not easy to attain. Many jobs are not socially acceptable to someone who has undergone a lengthy period of scholastic training. Others are far too demanding both in terms of time and mental and nervous energy. And if a decent salary is expected, it is only natural for the employer to expect his money's worth. Many jobs and professions are immediately closed to a person who intends to do some part-time ministry.

A rather different kind of drawback is the comparative lack of opportunity to carry on one's Christian witness within certain jobs. For instance, some have taken on forms of social work alongside their local Church ministry and have discovered that it is professionally unacceptable to use their contacts as a means of evangelism.

While those within the full-time ministry of the Church chafe because they see most of their energies being directed in shepherding the faithful and propping up the ecclesiastical structures, others have been equally frustrated by the comparative lack of direct evangelistic opportunity in part-time service. Maybe such a tension is inevitable. At least one should be aware that it exists.

In the nature of things we tend to draw our Christian leaders from among those who can spend most time on the job. Even with the recent growth in part-time ministries this still remains true.

However, a new factor is emerging – sometimes called the new leisure. A hundred years ago the average worker spent about 68 hours every week on his job. Today that figure has dropped to around 37 hours, and is still falling. Experts in this field say it will drop even further, the day not being far distant when we shall be spending up to four days a week away from our jobs.

Naturally this has tremendous implications for the Church's ministry. The number of full-timers and part-timers is a relatively small minority within the Church, probably not reaching more than about one per cent of the total membership. While it is not suggested that everybody is going to have more than half a week of leisure time if the present trend continues it will mean a vast increase in the number of hours that some Christians could spend in what we may describe as 'spare-time' Christian service.

But is the Church geared to take advantage of this potential? The sad fact is that frequently churches only wake up to the new situations after they have changed. We react to, rather than anticipate, new developments. We start building our Church on a new housing estate months after people have settled in their new homes. We send our first missionaries overseas long after the enterprising traders have pioneered the way. Yet it will be a sad waste of time and manpower if we fail to anticipate the changing pattern of leisure in our society.

Mark you, to be fair, it has to be pointed out that as yet this dramatic growth in leisure has not had so much effect on the white-collar workers, the executives, the professions.

That creates a problem, because it is largely from these areas of our society that the Church in Britain recruits its members.

Some of those who have retired and have used their increased leasure show a few of the ways in which the Church could be ready to capitalise on the released talents of those who want to use the time on their hands in the service of God.

One man I knew retired early after serious heart trouble, and then proceeded to spend hours every week visiting people in need. Little wonder his vicar regarded him as a literal 'god-send'. Between them they were able to cover effectively a large housing estate.

Another man bought himself a second-hand printing machine for a song. He installed it in his garage. After spending many hours working on it, he is in business printing for local Churches.

A man with a particular interest in a Missionary Society became an acceptable deputation speaker in his local area.

Some have taken up letter-writing as a ministry. It would be impossible to count the numbers of lonely people who have been cheered by receiving a letter from them. Many missionaries, too, have had cause to thank God for them, for after the first flood of enthusiastic supporters' letters has dried up, the few letters that arrive regularly are all the more valued. And if you think that letter writing is so common place that it does not merit being described as Christian service, then think again. Paul was a great letter writer, and imagine how much poorer the Church would be had he considered it beneath his dignity, or regarded himself as being too busy to write his letters.

With a little thought and imagination you could multiply the above examples. The new leisure needn't be a problem if Christians see the opportunities for service it provides, and Churches encourage the use of individual's gifts in these ways.

Specialised functions

A recent look at a number of Christian workers who had all been trained at the same college revealed some interesting facts. Twenty-two per cent had become school teachers (mostly Religious Education specialists), 20 per cent had taken up pastoral work, 18 per cent had gone overseas, almost nine per cent had gone into business and the rest were divided variously between administration, deputation, social or medical work, and further study.

Whatever else such facts say to us, they remind us of the wide variety of specialised functions there are to be fulfilled as part of Christian service. That is both comfort and challenge. Comfort because no Christian need feel that there is little opportunity for the exercise of his particular gift. Challenge because no Christian has any right to excuse himself from Christian service on the basis that there is nothing he can do.

A very brief survey of some of the main types of Christian service available today should help to give you a picture of the exciting possibilities that present themselves to the Christian Church.

Start with what is normally called the *home pastoral ministry*. Although, as we've already seen, the status of the parson in society has suffered a drastic decline, there is still a great need for him.

Recent official reports have tended to cast doubts upon that need. The Paul report told the Anglican Church that they had more clergy than they could afford. The Baptists too produced a report which suggested that perhaps the number of ministers should be reduced to about 400, although this figure was not accepted, and the official esti-mate is that over 1,000 will be needed.

It may seem logical that a decline in the numerical strength of the Church should be matched by a similar reduction in numbers of clergy and ministers. But that seems to me to be dangerously like a counsel of despair. If we are to see a reversal in the decline in our Churches a bold and imaginative approach is surely necessary. In any case the current losses from the ministry by death, retirement, and resignation, are greater than the numbers being recruited.

The home ministry is a very demanding specialised func-tion because of the varied types of work involved.

The minister should be a PASTOR. Much more is in-volved here than simply routine visits on Church members. A standing joke among parsons is that a pre-requisite for the job is the ability to drink unending cups of tea, with or without sugar, ranging in colour from dishwater grey to bright orangey brown, and at the same time keep up an un-ending flow of cheerful small talk.

In fact pastoral work is a much more serious business. It will include routine calls; midnight emergencies; helping someone whose world has just fallen around their ears; straightening out eternal triangles; rebuking recalcitrant Church members; rejoicing in the birth of a child; consoling grief; challenging apathy; sitting at the bedside of someone critically ill; standing by the grave of someone inexplicably cut off in their prime.

In short, the pastor's job is to be present in all the varied experiences of life. And not only to be present, but to have the right word to say. A tall order?

Certainly. But we haven't finished yet. The minister should be an ADMINISTRATOR. Although deacons, elders, churchwardens are appointed to assist in the smooth running of a Church, the minister has to act as a kind of managing director. He must co-ordinate all the different parts of the Church's life, and where there are conflicting interests he must arbitrate. Many of the petty frictions that bedevil our Churches can be avoided by skilful administration.

You may have suffered, as I have, some of those business meetings that start late, and ramble on under a benign but bumbling chairman, until at length they yawn their way to a near midnight close. The good administrator will take the trouble to learn and practise the art of chairmanship.

Then again the minister needs to be a capable PREACHER/TEACHER.

Some men give an exhibition of dramatic oratory. Others stun their congregations with erudition. Some seem to be trying to flog their hearers into submission. Others frankly bore to tears.

Happy is the congregation which hears sermons and addresses it can understand; that are interesting; that are relevant; that are helpful; that are instructive; that are spiritually profitable.

As if all this were not enough, the minister should be equally adept in leading a men's meeting, an over-sixties club, and a youth fellowship. He should be just as much at home opening a sale of work, compèring a Sunday School party, or leading a retreat on the deepening of the spiritual life. He must be a first-rate evangelist, and a deep spiritual teacher. He must spend much time out amongst people, but he must not neglect his hours of prayer and study. He must always be available for people, but he must be a real family man.

And do you know what? You can actually find people who combine all, or at least most, of these gifts. Not just one or two people. Hundreds of them.

But it has become increasingly recognised that we often ask too much from one person. So there has been a growth in part-time ministries, where a man may limit himself to the exercise of his particular gifts, or team ministries where individuals with different gifts can complement one another.

When we start thinking of *overseas missionary work* the same picture of variety emerges.

In spite of what some people imagine, the days of the

white missionary complete with pith helmet and retinue of native porters has long since disappeared. But the need for missionaries has not.

If you doubt that, drop a line to Christians Abroad, 38 King Street, London, WC2E 8JT, or the Inter Varsity Fellowship, 39 Bedford Square, London, WC1B 3EY, who will send you a current list.

Just a random sampling of such a list produced the following needs: a primary school teacher for Pakistan, a secondary school teacher for Zaïre, a school secretary for India, a Bible teacher for Portuguese Guinea, a lecturer for Sudan, an evangelist for Iran, a pastor for Brazil, a nurse for Ghana, a business administrator for South Africa, a physiotherapist for Uganda, a doctor for Ethiopia, a surgeon for Bangladesh, an agriculturalist for Korea, a translator for Thailand, a journalist for Indonesia, an industrial evangelist for Japan, and a youth worker for Laos.

The list, as well as underlining the variety of needs and opportunities overseas, also indicates the emphasis being placed now upon professional qualifications.

If you think that all that's needed to be a missionary is a Bible under one arm and a concern for the conversion of the heathen (and the pith helmet of course), forget it. High standards of professional competence are demanded not just by the Missionary Societies, but more important still, by the countries overseas. Many areas are not open to you unless you have qualifications.

You may at present be involved in study and examinations for a particular profession, and are wondering what you should do because you are sure God is calling you overseas. The temptation – and sometimes our teaching on total dedication encourages this – is to throw up the training to satisfy the urgent enthusiasm to get going on something really worthwhile. Don't give up. Complete your professional training. Strive to do your best, to get the highest possible qualifications. That way you'll be more likely to find openings later in missionary work.

Another specialised function which is clearly recognised

by the New Testament is that of the *evangelist*. 'Some have special ability in winning people to Christ, helping them to trust him as their Saviour' (Eph. 4:11).

One of the problems of listing different forms of Christian service is that at once we notice how much they overlap. There are many men in the ministry, and many more overseas who are evangelists. Yet there are those for whom this is a special calling.

Funnily enough, although it is not uncommon for someone to announce 'I feel called to be a minister', or 'I feel called to be a missionary', you don't hear anyone say 'I feel called to be an evangelist'.

Usually 'A special ability in winning people to Christ' has to be shown first. In the nature of things, this normally means that one has to begin in a small way, and part-time. Frequently experience can be gained through organisations like National Young Life Campaign, Youth for Christ, and Operation Mobilisation, as well as in the local Church.

Needless to say an 'ability in winning people to Christ' must not be confused with simple enthusiasm. Although the latter is obviously necessary, evidence of lasting conversions through one's personal witness and public speaking are necessary before you can consider yourself an evangelist. Even on this score a word of caution is essential. Because you are keen to be an evangelist you may, in your over-anxiety to produce results, procure snap 'decisions' from people. It is terribly easy to ask all the right questions in such a way that people almost inevitably give the right answers, and you assume that conversion has taken place. Therefore evidence of *lasting* conversions is necessary.

Societies like The Evangelisation Society, Movement for World Evangelisation, and Scripture Union provide opportunities for full-time evangelists, and some independent evangelists have gained their early experience from such organisations. There are a few openings for evangelists in the major denominations, but again it is entirely dependent upon evidence of gift. Note too that there are very few evangelists who hold major crusades and who have large supporting organisations. The majority are far more humble than that.

An evangelist is, to put it bluntly, judged by results. Therefore there is no royal route of training or qualifications that can be outlined, although of course the more biblical and theological background that can be obtained the better.

Literature work provides wide scope for Christians with certain qualifications. The scope is wide because there are opportunities in this country and overseas, and because there are widely different jobs to be done.

To begin with there is the job of the writer. The well-stocked shelves of Christian bookshops in the country is clear evidence that there is no shortage of Christian writers. But ask most publishers and you will find that they are agreed that there is a shortage of *good* Christian writers!

A number of reasons can easily be given for this. Until recently little attempt has been made either to encourage or to train new writers. Frequently the Christian book-buying public has tended to go for books by 'big names' regardless of whether those individuals have had the ability to write well.

Then, too, demand tends to create supply – simple economics ensure that. Almost inevitably it is the good seller rather than the good writer that is in demand. Sadly, this often means that the more sensational the book, the more likely it is to be in demand.

What are undoubtedly needed today are Christians who are professional in their approach to writing. To gain professional experience you must spend a good deal of time and effort. And most Christians are so bound up in their local Church – the keener they are the more committed they are – and in the business of earning a living that very little time or energy is left for writing. Yet, as with everything else, time, practice, and consistent effort are essential.

No one can measure what a powerful influence well-written books by Christians could have. As the Evangelical Alliance's Commission on Evangelism said, 'the public

71

library could be a distribution agency for positive literature, if it could be produced'.

As well as the writer there is the publisher. Skills here range from editing to business management, from proof-reading to accounting, from searching for new writing talent to selling it, from buying art work to planning a promotion campaign. The publisher has the considerable responsibility of deciding to a degree what books the public shall read and therefore what influences shall be brought to bear on people's minds.

The skills of the bookseller too are varied, yet vital to the successful distribution of good Christian literature. He must not only be a salesman. He must also regard his task as a spiritual ministry – a tension that is not always easy to resolve.

While we are on the subject of mass communication, we may just note that *radio* should also be included as a specific function. Apart from professional involvement either as a performer, or as a producer there is little apart from the set periods of religious broadcasting that makes radio, or television, in Britain particularly Christian. This is not to say that Christians should not involve themselves in a career where they can ultimately have great influence on what people will hear and see.

Generally speaking, the societies that exist for broadcasting in this country actually are missionary societies beaming their programmes into areas that cannot be reached by regular missionaries.

Radio technicians, programme directors, writers, and managers are needed as well as staff to deal with any enquiries. However, it should be made clear that this is a relatively small enterprise at present, and of course highly specialised.

Youth work is specialised too. The full-time youth leader may work in an open youth club, and will deal with young people in some depth.

Some may wonder whether it is right to include this in a book on Christian service. Yet this can be a very valuable piece of evangelistic work. There is demand for such youth leaders in Churches where they can work alongside the minister, and with the growth we have already noted in the development of team ministries it is likely that demand for fully-trained youth leaders will grow.

For many years the pattern in the churches in the U.S.A. has been for each Church to have its team of specialists – its minister of music, its minister of youth, as well as its secretary, preacher, and pastor. A set-up like this takes full account of the different gifts that individuals have as well as the tendency towards specialisation in society as a whole. There are, however, few British Churches that are large enough to sustain more than a ghost of such a pattern.

The grouping of churches, and the setting up of team ministries, does allow for the appointment of specialists. Christian youth leaders, who have previously been limited to work in local authority clubs, now have the growing opportunity of service as part of the life of a group of local churches.

From the numbers quoted at the beginning of this chapter, it is clear that many Christians have seen school *teaching* as a specialised function worthy of their attention.

Although not without its opponents, the present educational scene in Britain provides for compulsory religious education. Such a situation obviously presents a challenge. If children are going to be subjected to teaching about the Christian faith it is of great importance that those who teach them should be convinced of the truth of what they teach.

The situation in some schools where assembly in the mornings and the lesson periods are taken by agnostics, humanists, or those who just don't care, is not merely unsatisfactory – it is dangerous. Dangerous to the teacher's own moral integrity if he has to teach what he doubts, or actively disbelieves. Dangerous to the children in whom an early scepticism may be born which will be very difficult to eliminate later on.

Religious education done in an interesting way by a fully convinced teacher will not reduce the importance of Sunday school work or the value of teaching in the home, but can be a very useful addition.

But a word of warning; a religious educational specialist is not primarily an evangelist. While he may have considerable moral and spiritual influences upon his pupils he must be careful not to abuse his position or transgress professionally accepted educational standards.

School teaching may, of course, lead on in a minority of cases to lecturing budding R.E. specialists. Spiritual maturity and academic attainment are both demanded in such an influential position.

Lecturing in Theological, Bible, and Missionary Training Colleges is another specialised aspect of teaching. Much more than the collection of theological degrees is necessary, although some sort of high academic achievement and specialisation is normally required.

Since such colleges exist for practical training as well as for the attainment of theoretical knowledge, lecturers are normally expected to have some experience of service as a minister or missionary.

Administration of Christian societies and organisations should be remembered too. A wide variety of specialised functions is available, depending very much on the type of organisation it is. From time to time top jobs are advertised, although many societies prefer to rely on personal recommendations. Nepotism isn't entirely unknown in these circles, and more than one leader in this realm has said to me 'It's not what you know, but *who* you know that matters'. Naturally someone with administrative gifts and probably with business experience is required. Also it is often insisted that the person should have had some practical experience of the work the society represents. For this reason you often find that the General Secretary of a missionary society, for instance, once served that society overseas.

As well as the so-called top jobs there are also the clerks, typists, packers, receptionists, and so on. And until many of the societies see the sense of sharing premises and facilities wherever possible, it is likely that the demand here will go on exceeding the supply.

Seldom does this aspect of Christian work receive the attention it deserves. How often, for instance, have you heard someone giving a talk on Christian vocation include secretaries in a headquarters job? Missionaries, yes. But the secretary who types the letters, or the clerk who makes out the monthly pay chit? There is something romantic about sacrificing a promising career for the ministry, but no one gets up and cheers when a much more lucrative post in business is sacrificed in order to serve in a Christian bookshop, or type away in a Christian office. Pity, because demand is steady.

The last specialised function I'm calling *welfare*. This can include employment by a local authority as a Social Worker or by the Home Office as a Probation Officer. However, it must be remembered that professional etiquette makes it difficult to carry out an active Christian witness in 'official' welfare work. A feeling of frustration can result for those who would feel at home in a more aggressively evangelistic setting.

But run your eye down the classified advertisement columns of almost any Christian newspaper and you will find appeals for many different kinds of welfare workers – a matron for a children's home, or residential staff for an old people's home maybe. In addition, fully-trained officers of both the Church Army and the Salvation Army are engaged in a wide variety of welfare occupations.

The demand for the right kind of person is considerable, and although professional qualifications are frequently expected, even more important is a sense of Christian calling.

PART THREE
EQUIPMENT FOR SERVICE

Gifts

Have you ever heard that pious phrase, 'If the Lord calls He will equip'? There is some truth in it – but only some.

God can give you a special gift after He has called you for a particular job, yet I seriously doubt whether this is normal.

You may think that in the case of Jeremiah He did. After all, didn't He first call him to be a prophet, and then say to him, 'See I have put my words in your mouth! Today your work begins . . . ' (Jer. 1:9, 10)? But if you only read those two verses you're missing the point of the passage. Go back to verses four and five. There you read, 'The Lord said to me "I knew you before you were formed within your mother's womb; before you were born I sanctified you and appointed you as my spokesman to the world".'

In other words, God's call to Jeremiah depended on his total knowledge of him. And that surely means that God had already implanted certain gifts and abilities within Jeremiah which would be needed later and developed in his prophetic work. Jeremiah was not necessarily aware of his gifts at the time. On occasions it may seem that God bestows gifts after He calls, but what in fact is much more likely is that He calls on the basis of latent gifts we already possess. Often it is only after God has called us that we become aware of the gifts that are needed, and we see that these gifts we already have.

Looked at from the other point of view, a discovery of

the gifts we possess may well help us in deciding what God wants us to do. I think there is a sense in which this process of discovering our latent gifts can go on throughout life. Psychologists tell us that we only use a proportion of our abilities, and it should be an exciting experience finding what God has given us. Chad Varah of the Samaritans says that God's call to us is really a challenge to find out what we are for, and he adds that he did not find this out for himself until he was 42.

A good deal has been written and said in recent years about gifts. But it is almost exclusively to do with 'spiritual' gifts – faith, healing, miracles, the word of wisdom, the word of knowledge, discerning of spirits, prophecy, tongues, and interpretation. In this book we are concerned with what we might call 'natural' gifts, although with no intention of belittling 'spiritual' ones.

They are 'natural' in the sense that everyone has some of them. However, the power of God's Spirit is needed to make full use of them. We may discover our natural gifts and use them for our own selfish purposes, but in the end this is self-defeating. Not only does it fail to make the maximum use of our gifts, but it also leads to an impoverishment of our personality.

Later on we shall be looking at ways in which we can assess our own gifts. For the moment we shall make some attempt at a broad analysis.

First of all there are the people who are good at *doing* things. They are people who are never happier than when they are active. I don't necessarily mean by that the sort of person who is never still, dashing hither and thither, always on the go.

Jeremiah's potter was a 'doer' although he probably seldom moved from his pottery. We shouldn't confuse a sedentary person with someone who doesn't like doing things.

A pastor needs to be a 'doer', because he should like to be out and about among people. He may have a variety of other gifts as well which will put him in one of the other categories, but fey of us have gifts entirely from one group. However, normally one type of gift is uppermost and will therefore tend to shape our lives.

If your greatest enjoyment is found in tinkering with engines you are probably basically a doer. On the other hand if your real interest is in something very different – say painting pictures, you are still probably a doer.

Sometimes this is where we make a big mistake in our Churches. Have you ever been on the receiving end of a rousing, challenging sermon on the subject of witness, for instance? No one at the end can be in any doubt at all that it is the job of every Christian to witness. So far so good. The problem comes if the serman is being used to challenge us to engage in a particular form of witness – say door-to-door visitation. As a method of witness it is time-honoured and excellent. In a limited kind of way, it can be done by everyone. But to be done effectively it needs someone who is a doer. So what is the use of berating a congregation and making every non-doer feel guilty for not taking their share?

Funnily enough we are quick to recognise that it needs special gifts to preach, but we don't also see that different types of evangelistic enterprise require different types of gifts.

I suppose one of the classic examples of a doer in the New Testament is Martha (Luke 10). In our sermons we often paint her in a rather unfavourable light, but whatever mistakes she may or may not have made she was the practical one, the one who like Dorcas in Acts was full of good works – a doer.

The second board classification is the group we shall call the *teachers* – although we must be careful not to limit this simply to those who are in the teching profession.

Say the word 'teacher' and the majority of people will think in terms of someone imparting knowledge or information. But cast your mind back to your school days. Every teacher had knowledge and information to impart. They passed it on to you, but by no means all of it stuck. That may have been due to a lack of interest on your part but in many cases it was simply because the person teaching you was not a true 'teacher' – he did not have the power to communicate effectively.

It is interesting to note that some careers psychologists say that an important element in teaching is salesmanship. In other words it's more than simply imparting information. That information has to be put over in such a way that the learner is interested, and persuaded to accept it.

Obviously we come very close here to many aspects of Christian work. The preacher, the evangelist, the missionary, all are teachers – not in the narrow sense of injecting a sterile body of beliefs into the wooden heads of their hearers, but in the sense that they have something of terrific importance to communicate. And that communication has to be done in such a way that their hearers will both understand and accept it.

If, then, a teacher is a salesman, so is the Christian preacher, witness or evangelist. Does that shock you? Only because you have come to associate salesmen with words like slick, 'hot sell', high-powered, and that dirtiest of all words for the Christian – money. Yet all of us spend a great deal of our lives selling ourselves if nothing else. We persuade others to trust us, to believe in our abilities. We have to, to survive. Salesmanship in this broad sense must be part of the gift of the teacher. Not that the preacher or evangelist should be slick, or should try 'hot sell' methods. Far from it. But he does have more than information to impart. He does need to be able to communicate his message effectively.

The teacher may, of course, be a doer as well. But it is highly unlikely that he will be equally good at both.

Although it is true that these categories overlap, it is as well for you to discover where you are strongest.

The third category is the *organisers*.

Most business organisations are so structured that power is in the hands of the organisers. The career structure is such that promotion leads from the doers at the bottom up to the organisers at the top. And because most people, for economic and status reasons, want promotion, each must be prepared to be an organiser.

This is a very dangerous situation. For one thing it can easily mean that someone who is a brilliant doer becomes an inefficient organiser simply because he expects and deserves promotion. Even worse, it implies that the person with 'doing' gifts is necessarily inferior to the person with organising gifts.

Fashions change, it's true. There was a time when a particular class of 'doer' – the entertainer – was frowned upon in our society. Now he is looked up to in a way that is out of all proportion to his contribution to society.

I simply mention this to underline the fact that we have not necessarily moved 'up' a grade when we talk about organisers in Christian service. There is undoubtedly a need for those who have gifts of organisation, who have management ability within the Christian Church. To say this does not mean that I'm advocating that we should ignore the Holy Spirit. The moment you talk about 'management' or 'administration' some Christians get terribly worried in case you are becoming unspiritual. But 'God is not one who likes things to be disorderly and upset. He likes harmony' (1 Cor. 14:33).

Time and space does not allow me to recount at length the sorry tale of film meetings when the projector wouldn't work, or the film had not turned up, or business meetings for which no agenda had been prepared, or services for which no speaker – or maybe two speakers – had been booked, or chairmen who bungled, or preachers who couldn't be heard, or choirs that hadn't been trained, or magazines that had more blank pages than blotchy ones, of notice boards that hadn't been stripped of last year's announcements, of pews that have no more than an infrequent nodding acquaintance with a duster, of church kitchens that appear to have no drains – I won't bore you with the sordid details. A recital of the failures, the disorganisation, the disarray of the Church would be almost endless. We need leaders with gifts of administration and organisation.

One more group of gifts belong to the *'dreamers'*. I think some of the Old Testament prophets, and the writers of some of the Psalms were dreamers. Martha's sister probably came into this category too, and maybe the Apostle John. These people seemed to have the time and inclination to see visions and dream dreams.

Once again this category may overlap with others. A few may be able to put their dreams into operation. Others may at least be able to communicate their dreams to others who can turn them into reality.

But before you start slapping yourself heartily on the back and congratulating yourself that you are above all else a dreamer, let me warn you that ours is a harshly practical world that tends to ignore the visionary, and certainly doesn't pay him well.

As a schoolboy I had no patience with poetry. I liked adventure stories. I liked practical things. Until I met a teacher who not only revelled in poetry, but had the ability to convey some of his enthusiasm to his pupils.

Generally speaking the poet, the visionary writer, the profound artist, the spiritual prophet is understood and accepted by a tiny minority. Yet perhaps there was never an age that was more in need of them – particularly the Christian prophet and dreamer. Faced by the onslaught of materialism and secularism, Western Christianity has tended to become defensive. Growing inward-looking it has concentrated in self-preservation, or crude head-counting proselytism.

I know that Jesus was a very practical man – a doer if ever there was one. I know too that there has never been a finer teacher. He was obviously a great organiser and leader of men. But He was a dreamer too. No one who chose 12 peasants to form the basis of a world-wide Church could be other than a dreamer.

Jesus, too, is a clear warning that being a dreamer is no soft option. It demands every bit as much hard work as any other group of gifts. When someone is employed in industry or commerce as an 'ideas' man it is assumed that he is being paid a fat wage for sitting in a plush office and doing nothing except allowing ideas to pop out automatically now and again. The 'ideas' man knows that this is far from the truth.

I've used this illustration of the 'ideas' man in a commercial setting for a purpose. In a lowly sense he too is a dreamer. He may only be dreaming up new ways of advertising a particular brand of toothpaste, but he is trying to use his mind in such a way that he catches a vision of something which is to be passed on to a public who will then want to buy the product.

The trouble is that when we talk about seeing visions and dreaming dreams we imagine that it's all so airy-fairy. But when Amos had a vision of a basket of ripe fruit (chapter 8) it had a very practical and down-to-earth application. Israel was ripe for punishment because the poor were oppressed and cheated and enslaved (verses 4-6). And when Jeremiah saw, 'a pot of boiling water tipping southward, spilling over Judah' (Jer. 1:13) it was a practical warning, not only of a coming invasion, but also of the direction from which it would come.

Perhaps the most famous of all dreamers was Joseph. His brothers – all practical to a man – despised him for it, but they were to discover the importance of practical dreams.

Often we just don't allow the prophet, the dreamer, the visionary to develop in our Churches. He isn't seen to be useful enough. We lay great store by the person who is active, who is always waving a full diary at you, who packs every 24 hours with what we call 'living'. We set a premium on busyness, on results that can be quantified, on achievements that hit the headlines, on work that brings immediate dividends. And dreams fly out of the window. Because real dreams (as opposed to your commercial type idea) demand time and patience, prayer and waiting.

If I've spent a long time emphasising the dreamer it's because we need him urgently, and because I believe Arthur O'Shaughnessy was quite right when he said, 'One man with a dream, at pleasure, shall go forth and conquer a crown'.

Assessing your gifts

Now to be more specific. It is one thing to know into which general category of gift yours fall, but quite another to know what particular gift or gifts God has given you. Or perhaps even more important is the discovery of one's *best* gifts, for it is surely these that God wants us to use primarily.

A mistake that is sometimes made among Christians is to think it unspiritual to develop and use one's greatest gifts. I remember a young man who was undoubtedly a highly gifted musician throwing up his music and turning to commerce because he regarded it as consecration to do so. He may have been right to do so if he had an even greater gift to exercise, but it usually seems to be the case that people get a fixed idea of what consecration involves in terms of giving up things, and as a result are in danger of falling into the same trap as the man in the parable who lost his talent because he didn't use it.

If God has given us gifts –and everyone of us has received something – it must be part of our responsibility to discover what those gifts are and then develop them to the full. We may not necessarily like the gifts God has given us. I may be a doer when I would like to be a dreamer, or a teacher when I would prefer to be an organiser. However, over that none of us has any control. The gifts are part of God's equipment for service in life, and if we are going to be useful to God and at the same time find our own self-fulfilment, then we must assess our own gifts as accurately as possible.

Some of us have no problems here. Our gifts are obvious. If you are in this happy position you can skip this chapter.

For the rest, we'll start with a personal survey. And for this I suggest that you turn back to chapter three. There I listed five tests to discover whether or not you had received a call to some form of Christian service. The same tests, applied differently, will help to highlight your gifts.

1. *Are there things I am interested in and particularly like doing?* Psychologists professionally concerned with career guidance tell us that 'your aptitudes should follow your interests'. That is another way of saying that the things you like are normally the things you are good at. So get a piece of paper and list the things you are interested in. At this stage don't worry whether or not you can see any relation to Christian service. That can come later.

List everything – hobbies as well as the more formal subjects. Try to give some sort of preference rating, even if this means that all your hobbies come out on top.

Put down things you are interested in, even if you have never actually tried them. Take preaching as an example. You may have been under the misapprehension that you mustn't attempt this unless you are quite certain of a call to it. How then are you to discover whether or not you are gifted in this direction? You will probably not find it possible or wise to start by expecting to give a full sermon in a Church service. But there are other ways of starting – a school debating society, a Christian Union, a firm's dinner, for example, can give you some taste of speaking in public.

2. *Is there any external evidence that I am good at any of the things I have already listed?*

There should be. But make sure that the evidence is accurate and honest. It is possible to have listed under 1. some things that you would like to be interested in rather than things you are actually interested in.

For instance, you may have a romantic dream of becoming a writer. You like the idea. You are certainly interested in literature. But can you do it? Is there any evidence in your school work that you have a potential in this direction. School essays are a far cry from a literary masterpiece, I know, but they can reveal whether or not you have a feel for words and can clearly and cogently express yourself. It might be worthwhile asking your teachers what they think.

Make sure that any evidence in the form of opinions from your fellow Christians is honest. I don't mean that we are intentionally dishonest, but we are rightly afraid of unnecessarily hurting someone. So it's possible to preach an utterly boring sermon and still find people saying 'Thank you for your message', as they shake your hand afterwards. So find someone who is prepared to be frank with you.

Then, just as you made an attempt to put your interests in some sort of order of preference, try too to rank the things you're good at.

3. *Do I have any conviction that God wants me to use one or more of the gifts on my list?*

The simple act of putting these things down on paper will help to clarify your thinking. At this point it may become crystal clear that there is a particular gift that stands out from all the rest. The strong likelihood is that God wants you to major on that one.

Even if one does not stand out like this, prayer may indicate that there is one you should concentrate on

4. *Am I prepared to wait, and put my gifts to the test?*

A large part of the Christian life seems to be made up of learning to wait. No. 3 won't necessarily come all in a rush. Conviction is like a plant. It can be forced, but it will normally be a weak specimen if it is.

5. *Is God providing opportunities for the use of my gifts?*

This is important. Gifts are not given to us in isolation. We have them as a trust to be used within the Church and the world for the glory of God.

We may have gifts which are in abundance at the moment, and which therefore God does not want us to develop. On the other hand we may possess latent gifts of which we are at present unaware which are greatly needed, and for which God will provide the means both for their discovery and their development.

Therefore we need to be sensitive to God's guiding. If He closes the way in front of us then it is probably because there is some other work for us to do and gift for us to exercise.

This leads us on to another important point in making an accurate personal survey. Having gone through the five stages mentioned above we may still not be clear what our particular gift or gifts are. Or we may have found some gifts the use of which God has not confirmed. We are therefore left with the possibility of there being some latent gift which we have so far missed, or a gift we have discovered about which we have insufficient evidence to make us confident of its use.

Relax. A tremendous talent may be staring you in the face, and you've never noticed it. Or it may be just below the surface. A little scratching may bring it to light.

Look back over your life. Has anyone ever said to you 'You've got a talent for that'? But you have long since forgotten it. Or was there something you used to do – or for that matter still do – that you really like and are good at?

I know a young fellow who was good at art early on in his schooling. Then he made some mistakes. His art teacher laughed at him and he lost interest in the subject. Years later when he was rummaging around in his subconscious he remembered this long forgotten talent, and renewed his interest in it.

You may have hints like that. Or you may have heard someone say to you 'You'd make a good preacher' or 'One day you'll be a doctor'. At the time you hadn't a clue why they said it, so you put it out of your mind. Now you remember it and put it down on paper. It may be important.

Personal surveys like this can throw up all kinds of interesting facts about you. However, advice from others can also be useful in assessing your gifts.

We've already mentioned seeking the advice of fellow Christians, but it can often be of value to gain the opinion of someone who has professional experience in this area.

Career Plan, 7 Wine Office Court, London, EC4 3BY,

for instance, is a Christian organisation designed primarily to act as an employment agency for suitable Christians who require jobs in banking, insurance and similar professions in London. However, they also have a small department that specialises in career guidance and this could be useful to you.

A secular organisation that you should not overlook is the Vocational Guidance Association, Ulster Place, Upper Harley Street, London, N.W.1. Begun in 1954 it claims to help more than 4,000 people every year.

Although undergoing the series of sophisticated tests is not cheap, it should prove invaluable if you are still in any doubt about where your gifts lie.

One of the advantages of a secular organisation of this kind is that it takes a totally objective look at you. You may have to make a certain adjustment to apply their findings to a spiritual calling, but even the act of doing that is useful. The use of an objective study like this can also help us to avoid some of our personal preconceptions about what is or is not spiritual.

'But,' you may say, 'this is terribly unspiritual. Surely God can show me what my gifts are without the expense of going through some secular agency which bases its judgements on psychology. If I pray to Him, He will guide me.'

Perfectly true. But it is surprising how often God uses human means to accomplish His will. The same thing happens in other spheres. He *can* provide us with a large sum of money to buy a house 'out of the blue' so to speak. More often He enables us to get it in the more conventional way of a mortgage through a building society.

Equally He may give us a clear awareness of our gifts without any help. But if that is not how He does it for us, we should feel no sense of guilt if we consult a thoroughly well-proved and professional organisation that will be able to offer its advice and expertise.

While we are at this business of self-assessment it is a good idea to note any weak spots. A professional career organisation will tell you the general areas in which your

87

score was low. For instance it may tell you that your aptitude for administration is very low. That is important because it means that you should be careful to avoid any calling that is primarily administrative.

However, an awareness of your weaknesses has another value. It may be that the particular job you have to do, while not primarily administrative includes some administration. This need not mean that you should not tackle the job. Certainly it means that you should do everything possible to strengthen your strong points to compensate for this weakness, but also that you should make every effort to eliminate your weakness.

You may be surprised at the results. Probably you've heard of people who've had no schooling who have concentrated on that weak spot, overcome it, and become great scholars.

Or take Disraeli, whose maiden speech in the House of Commons was hooted at and shouted down. Even his best friends recognised what a miserable flop it had been and mentally wrote him off as a budding politician. But Disraeli wasn't beaten. He set about the difficult task of remedying his weakness. In the end he mastered the art of speaking until people were forced to listen to him.

Although in a different context, Paul, too, had discovered the truth of this, for he wrote 'when I am weak, then I am strong – the less I have, the more I depend on Him' (2 Cor. 12:10).

The qualities you will need

At this point we must make a brief detour.

So far I have tried to answer practical questions about Christian service and to provide as much information as possible. This is not supposed to be a devotional book. There are plenty of those on the market.

However, I wouldn't want anyone to go away with the impression that gift and training are so important that character can be neglected. In fact, character is in certain respects far more important in Christian work than a person's gifts or examination qualifications.

So we must spend a few pages looking at the qualities of character you will need. I'm not proposing to give a complete picture of the Christian's character, but there are certain qualities that we have every right to seek in a leader, whatever his walk of life, and in particular in a Christian leader.

Without question, *humility* should characterise the Christian worker. The message is as clearly for us as it was for Baruch, 'Are you seeking great things for yourself? Don't do it' (Jer. 45:5).

You might be forgiven for thinking that this should go without saying, but sadly it is not so. Even a man as greatly used as John Wesley has been described by Dr Albert Outler as being 'as proud as Lucifer'. Many lesser men have deserved a similar description.

Part of the problem is that we tend to be infected, even as Christians, with the prevailing attitudes of our age. And Vance Packard was right when he described so many as the 'status seekers'. Even the modern lust for more money and all the things it can buy is very largely a matter of looking for the status money and possessions bring rather than the actual material objects themselves.

In Church life this reveals itself in several ways. There is the minister who looks for a bigger Church ostensibly because he feels he should do a more 'significant' job, but in reality because the bigger the Church he runs, the more respect he gains from ordinary people. And the reverse is true. If he stays in a small Church he may be thought of by some as not having made the grade, and by the less kind as being a total failure.

Or there is the administrator of a Christian organisation who falls into the current management pattern of many commercial concerns in regarding his subordinates as cogs in his machine.

Whatever gifts such leaders may have, and they may be considerable, they have forgotten the basic truth that Jesus taught 'Anyone wanting to be a leader among you must be your servant. And if you want to be right at the top, you must serve like a slave' (Matt. 20:26, 27).

The gifts required for Christian leadership are often identical with those demanded for secular leadership. The attitudes are entirely different.

Maturity should be another characteristic of the Christian leader. This has nothing necessarily to do with age. We have already seen that age – at either end of the scale – is no bar to Christian service. In fact, the majority of training colleges do set a minimum age for their students in the hope that to some extent this will ensure maturity.

Psychological maturity and physical age should progress together. However they don't always do so. I have met some young people who, as the saying goes, have an old head on young shoulders. On the other hand I could introduce you right now to others in middle age or beyond who betray a strangely immature attitude to life. All of us are really a mixture of mature and immature elements, and that is perfectly normal. There is nothing wrong with occasionally letting down one's hair. Indeed the ability to relax and play without adult inhibitions would save us from many of the tensions that threaten our service. However, particularly in leadership situations, we need to be balanced on the side of maturity.

Even more important is spiritual maturity. Although Paul warned Timothy not to let anyone despise his youthfulness, he also said to him 'the pastor must not be a new Christian, because he might be proud of being chosen so soon, and pride comes before a fall' (Tim. 3:6). What is true for the pastor is true for any Christian leader.

If it is surprising that Churches by and large lay so much emphasis these days on youth in Christian service, it is alarming that so often little account is taken of a person's spiritual maturity. Yet a convert of a few months is unlikely to have the experience or knowledge necessary to give him leadership qualities. To force him into an intensive theological training is not likely to do him or the Church much good.

Much valuable Christian work has been begun but never completed because the person involved has lacked the grace of *stickability* or *stamina*.

Again this is required in the normal physical sense as well as in the spiritual.

Note the way Paul emphasises this truth. He reminds his young friend Timothy that he must be like a soldier, an athlete, and a farmer (2 Tim. 2:3, 5, 6). Each of these occupations demands patience, courage, and stamina. 'Stand steady' (2 Tim. 4:5) is not only good advice. It is essential.

Looking back over my own ministry I am convinced that one of the mistakes I have made is to be too ready to move on. I know that like Abraham we have to be prepared to pull up our roots if it becomes clear that God is calling us to do so. What is more 'even when he reached God's promised land, he lived in tents like a mere visitor . . . ' (Hebrews 11:9). There is an unquestionable danger in getting too settled and so failing to reach forward to exciting new challenges.

On the other hand we need to be quite sure that the job God has given us to do has been finished before we move on. Especially in Britain today there is need for greater stability. It is becoming the custom for people to be more mobile. Promotion in one's work often demands moving to another area. Large firms expect mobility in their staff. The result is an additional factor in the breakdown of the community – a breakdown that many experts feel to be contributing to family tensions, marriage problems, and health troubles.

A pastor who is able to stay for a fairly lengthy period in

one area can help to bring stability, and is more likely to do a lasting work. Equally he is more likely to see results for his efforts – an important factor for his encouragement. Often a minister will be given a tough assignment which leads him to depression. He moves on and almost at once blessing begins to come. Had he stayed just a few more months he would have rejoiced in that blessing. Instead he begins all over again in another tough assignment.

Most committees of missionary societies or of denominational ministry departments will expect you to give some evidence of having seen a job through.

It ought almost to go without saying that the candidate for a specialised function should have a regular and deep *devotional life*.

There are many books on the subject, so I do not need to stop and tell you how this should be cultivated. Let me simply emphasise its importance for the Christian in general but for the potential Christian leader in particular

The neglect of private prayer and reading of the Scriptures will guarantee spiritual barrenness and ultimately failure in one's particular service. The reason for this is simple. Christian work is spiritual work, and therefore demands spiritual power to accomplish it.

Of course you may neglect your devotional life and still run a busy and crowded church or a mission hospital that completes a record number of operations. But the Church will be little more than a social club and the hospital not a mission - unless of course there are others on the staff who are the channels of power through their prayer and Bible reading. If that is the case don't kid yourself that you are the leader in any more than name.

Spiritual blessing depends upon spiritual resources, which in turn depend on a healthy devotional life through which we keep in contact with God Himself.

A quality of a totally different sort is a *sense of humour*. I don't mean necessarily the ability to tell jokes. Nor do I mean the skilful weaving of funny stories into your sermons or talks. Rather, I have in mind the ability to laugh at yourself.

When we are in Christian work we are involved in serious business. Whatever particular aspect we are immediately concerned with, ultimately we are dealing with eternal issues. We cannot therefore have a frivolous attitude to what we are doing. Since we are involved with people and their well-being, their needs, their destinies, we are bound to need a sense of responsibility about it.

At the same time there is a danger in taking ourselves too seriously. 'But', you say, 'I've heard of some of the great Christian leaders who have wept over people. And didn't Jesus weep over Jerusalem? Isn't this the way into blessing?'

Well, yes and no. True, on one occasion Jesus wept over the city, but we do not gain the impression that he was always, or even often, doing this. On the other hand he talked about people who saw a speck of sawdust in some-one else's eye but didn't notice a great plank sticking out of their own (Matt. 7:3–5), and about the Pharisees, who with great care strained out a gnat that had fallen into their cup, but didn't notice the camel, and swallowed it. We can almost hear the ordinary people having a good chuckle.

The point is that Jesus had both a sense of humour and a deep concern for the people that made him weep. He didn't spend his time in rollicking laughter or joke-telling, time was too short. But nor did he spend his time weeping. He knew the wisdom of the ancient writer who said there is 'A time to cry: a time to laugh' (Eccl. 3:4).

We often hear the phrase 'the balance of power' as being an essential ingredient in international peace. A sense of balance in Christian things is more important than we often allow. The Christian can very easily become tense, frustrated, anxious and overburdened simply because he loses this essential balance. He lays too much emphasis on one thing at the expense of something quite different and equally important, so he becomes lop-sided.

The word 'heretic' literally means someone who is lop-sided in doctrine, but even if we can claim to be thoroughly orthodox in our beliefs we have to watch out that we do not become heretics in our behaviour. Of course our work as Christians is serious. Of course there is a need to weep over sin – our own and other people's. But there is also a place for a sense of humour, and in particular for the ability to laugh at one's self.

Whatever the specialised function you undertake, there will be times when circumstances look pretty forbidding, or when colleagues are particularly irritating, or when our work appears more than usually frustrating. Then especially you will need the grace of humour. You will be surprised what a rich gift of God it can be.

Perhaps another characteristic that ought to go without saying is a *love for people*. I mention it not only because of its importance, but also because of its frequent absence.

When a Christian has a genuine care and love for people he cannot hide it. It is one of the things that speaks most loudly about him and is most likely to commend Christ to others.

But they sense it too if our love is not really directed at them personally. It is so easy to imagine that we love people when in reality we love those who think pretty much the same as we do, or have a roughly similar social background. Also possible is the sort of love that is really no more than a disguised wish for converts – the passion for souls, as it used to be described – or at least for the potential hearers of our sermons.

You can't love potential converts. You can't love possible pew fillers. You can't even love people en masse. Love, to mean anything at all, must be deep and intensely personal. It must be between you and individuals.

PART FOUR
PREPARING FOR SERVICE

Making a start

Assuming that you believe that God is calling you to some specific function, the next step is to make some sort of start in preparing yourself. Whatever your future is likely to be, the best you can do is have a talk with your vicar, minister, or some other trusted leader within your Church, right at the very beginning.

You may be hesitant to do this, in case you are committing yourself too soon, but for most Christian work it is essential. If you are hoping to do some form of professional work it is not so necessary in the early stages, but even then, if you are going to regard it as a vocation which is a specific response to God's will for your life, you would do well to talk it over with someone with leadership responsibilities within your own Church.

If it is either the home ministry or the overseas mission field that is your interest, it is essential that you should gain the support of your own Church and its leaders. They will be required to recommend you for training, so the sooner you make known your desire to them the better.

As far as professions like teaching or social work are concerned, you will need to make the normal approaches for training demanded by that career. Information can be obtained from careers books in your local library.

For the pastoral ministry in this country you will need to find out your own denomination's application procedure. Each has its well-defined regulations which are in some instances as strict as any other profession. For this reason you should ask your vicar or minister to put you in touch with the relevant department at the denominational headquarters.

For instance, a candidate for ordination in the Anglican Church must first contact his Diocesan Director of Ordinands, who will arrange for all necessary interviews. Before he can begin his training he must be sponsored by a diocesan bishop and recommended by the Bishop's Selection Conference, which is arranged by the Advisory Council for the Church's Ministry (A.C.C.M.). Normally a candidate is expected to have passed at least two 'A' level G.C.E.s and to proceed to a university degree, although the particular course is decided in conjunction with the bishop. Very full information is given in a series of excellent booklets which can be obtained from A.C.C.M., Church House, Dean's Yard, London, SW1P 3NZ.

The Methodist route to ordination is equally defined. First you must be accepted as a Local Preacher, and pass the requisite examinations. Next you must be nominated by your Superintendent Minister at the Quarterly Meeting. This is followed by a series of examinations and interviews, until final approval by the Connexional Candidates Examination Committee, and the Methodist Conference. You will then be sent to a Methodist Training College.

The procedures for the United Reformed Church are similar. The candidates must be approved by the local Church and then the District Council before being allowed to attend a national Assessment Conference. This is followed by the Ministerial Committee of the Provincial Synod. Only after satisfactorily negotiating this course can you be accepted by a Theological College.

Other denominations have somewhat similar patterns of approval for their ministry and you should make yourself aware of them.

Procedures like these may seem like so much red tape, but you have to remember that each denomination has the responsibility of screening every applicant. Their job is to make sure that as far as possible no one gets as far as spending three or more years in college unless there is clear evidence of a call from God. Committees may make mistakes and approve the wrong people, and reject those who later turn out to be great leaders. Yet some sort of machinery has to be put into operation to keep out the misguided, the mistaken, or the plain cranks. In any case, as we've already seen, the Church has a definite responsibility to fulfil in encouraging and recognising the call of God. And a person like Gladys Aylward will come through anyway, whether turned down or not by a committee.

Those who wish to be missionaries will have to go through a series of procedures too. These vary from society to society, and so I can do no more than lay down the broad principles.

You may approach the matter by deciding for a variety of reasons that God wants you to work in a particular part of the world. You may have seen a film, or met a missionary from a certain country, or inexplicably always had a fascination for that area. If this is how it works out for you, the next step is to find out which societies work in that area and, if there are several, which one is closest to you in outlook and purpose.

Or perhaps you are drawn to a particular missionary society: in which case the area you will serve in will be secondary, and will be decided probably in conjunction with the society, bearing in mind their current needs.

Whichever approach you take, it is important to make as early a contact with the missionary society as you can. The candidates' secretary will be able to give you invaluable advice on the professional qualifications and experience you should obtain, on books you should read, on suitable colleges you may consider, and the necessary procedures for your adoption as a candidate. A lot of wasted time and effort can be avoided by making such an early contact, even though at this stage you are not making a formal application.

Talking of applications, this is the point at which to say something about how to go about making the right approach to a missionary society or denominational department.

At the end of this chapter there is a typical sample of the sort of form that will face you at some stage during your application. For the moment we will deal with the initial letter and interviews.

First impressions are important. Candidates' Secretaries and committees are primarily interested in discovering whether or not you are called by God to a specific function. Yet, being human, they will to some extent be governed by the kind of person you are.

Since first impressions are often the most lasting, it is as well for you to be thoroughly businesslike. Sadly, by no means all Christian organisations are in their turn efficient. Some will keep you waiting a long time for a decision, or even just an acknowledgement. But that is no excuse for you to be shoddy.

If possible type your letter. You have no idea of the problems people will have deciphering your handwriting, even when it's perfectly clear to you. If you have no access to a typewriter, at least print your name and address clearly.

Make sure too that the letter is clean and well laid out. Keep a copy for your own reference.

Take some trouble to find out the name and correct title of the right person to deal with your enquiry. Letters can take a long time being passed from one desk to another. In any case, it shows that you have taken that little bit of extra care.

In reply to your letter you may be sent forms to fill in. Do so carefully, fully, and honestly.

Or you may be asked for a c.v. or curriculum vitae. Don't be put off by the jargon. All they want is a brief outline of who you are – name, address, age, marital state – and of what you have done – school, college, jobs, qualifications.

The next major hurdle is the interview. This may be with an individual in the first place, or a committee, although increasing use is now being made of the residential type of interview where a panel can really get to know you in informal talks as well as in the more formal situation.

Whatever the type of interview you face, the approach is the same.

Arrive on time, even if this means sitting for some long, nail-biting minutes before you are ushered in.

Speak up. The interviewers genuinely want to hear what you have to say, and some of them may be a little deaf.

Be prepared to listen. Nerves tend to make us talk too much, and to be too impatient to hear the whole question.

Be calm. The grilling you are being given may make you suspect that you are being considered for a £10,000 a year job, but it is really because your interviewers are your friends. They are genuinely concerned for your well-being. They neither want you nor the Church to suffer from a misfit.

Don't give the impression that you know it all, or that you are God's greatest gift to the Church. You may imagine that you are another John Wesley or Gladys Aylward. Time alone will tell. At the moment you are just a very ordinary person who happens to believe that God wants you to do a job for Him.

Don't name-drop. Your interviewers may just be interested that you are on Christian name terms with a bishop, or that your great-uncle was in China with Hudson Taylor. But their real concern is to find out who you are, not who you know.

When it's all over and you've done your best, you may of course be turned down. Such a setback is naturally a disappointment, but it need not be a crushing one, since all along you should have been seeking God's will, and this in some way is simply a further working out of that.

Being turned down may be only a temporary setback designed to test your character. Perhaps you should try another society, or another specialised function.

Or it could be God's way of saying you must not go ahead in this direction at all. The reasons given for turning you down should be very carefully studied, as they may give you a clue to your next step.

Presuming that you have previously secured the approval of your Church, this is the point at which you should go back to talk it over further with them.

The following forms are reproduced by kind permission of the Church Missionary Society. Part I is for the initial approach, and Part II is for definite candidature.

1. Please give
    (a) Your full name
    (b) Present address
    (c) Telephone number
    (d) Permanent address (if different from above)
    (e) Home parish
    (f) Date and place of birth
    (g) Date and place of baptism
    (h) Date and place of confirmation

2. (For single candidates)
    Are you engaged or likely to become so in the near future?

3. (For married candidates)
    (a) Date of marriage
    (b) Maiden name (women)
    (c) Names of children, if any, and dates of their birth

4.   (a) Are your parents living?
    If so, where?
    Are they in sympathy with your wish to offer?
    Have you brothers and sisters?
    (b) Are you a British subject by birth?
    If not, give particulars.

5.   (a) Where were you educated and professionally trained?
    Please give names of schools and colleges, hospitals, etc. with dates.
    (b) What examinations have you passed and what degrees and diplomas have you taken?
    Give your qualifications in full.

6.   What has been your occupation since leaving school or college?
      Give details.
7.   (a) What are your recreations and amusements?
      (b) Have you studied any foreign language?
      If so, to what extent?
      Do you consider that you have any linguistic aptitude?
      Would you be prepared to learn a language?
8.   (a) Is any relative dependent upon you for support, wholly or in part, or likely to become so?
      (b) Have you any provision for sickness or old age?
      (c) Do you have any other financial commitments?
      (d) Are you a member of any Superannuation Scheme?
9.   (a) If you have ever been a member of any other branch of the Church, please say which it was and why you left it.
      (b) What place of worship do you attend, and what is the name of your Vicar?
10.   Have you ever offered your services to any other Missionary Society?

PART II

1. Describe briefly the beginning and development of your Christian faith.
2. How are you trying to express your Christian vocation in your present situation?
3. What career prospects are open to you at present?
4. How did your interest in work overseas arise?
5. What is your reason for wishing to go overseas?
6. (a) What do you consider to be the most significant experience in your life to date?
   Why is it significant to you?
   (b) What do you think are your major strengths and weaknesses?

Where do you think your main difficulties lie?
7. What do you think it means to be a Christian?
8. Mention any problems you may have in your Christian faith.
9. (a) What is your practice in regard to:—
    Bible Study?
    Prayer?
    Holy Communion?
    (b) Please tell us of any ways in which your practice relating to them has helped you in your spiritual life recently.
10. What kind of books, papers and periodicals do you read? Mention any books which have specially helped you and say why.
11. How do you interpret God's call to you as regards length of service overseas?

It should also be remembered that in addition to the form filling and the interviews you will be required to undergo a medical examination.

Where can you train?

Once you enter college it is very difficult to get out. All the pressures see to that. There are financial pressures like the local education authority's grant, or the gifts of your home Church. Who are you to throw these back at them?

There are family pressures. Having convinced your people of the need to obey a sense of vocation, it isn't easy to justify a drastic change in mid-course.

Then there are personal pressures. Considerable humility

is required to admit to your friends, or for that matter to yourself, that you made a mistake.

There are theological pressures too – all that about putting the hand to the plough, and not looking back.

So it is important to be sure on two counts. The first of these is whether or not you should go to a Theological or Bible College at all. Since most courses are two or three years long you obviously won't want to spend your time or money to no account.

Some regard attendance at a college simply as a means of further education. If you are interested in collecting a series of degrees or diplomas, then by all means get fixed up at a Theological or Bible college. But these colleges are designed primarily to train those who want to prepare for specialised Christian functions. I doubt whether the collection of unnecessary academic qualifications can be regarded as Christian stewardship.

A problem which faces most colleges from time to time is the person who applies simply because they have failed at everything else. But there is a great deal more to the courses offered by the colleges listed here than pure academic teaching. There is practical training, some form of community living, and spiritual discipline. To endure, much less profit from, such a many-sided course you need to have been a success rather than a failure in your present job.

Having made quite certain that you need to go to a training college in order to prepare for some type of Christian ministry the next thing you want to be certain about is which college.

The list that follows does not claim to be completely comprehensive, but it does cover the majority of colleges in Britain. Although all of them are functioning at the time of writing, there have been closures in recent years. Probably more will close or combine with others in the immediate future.

Colleges differ widely in their churchmanship and theological outlook. As far as possible the note on this has been made using the colleges' own words in order to avoid bias.

Where no note has been made it is normally because, although there may be a theological emphasis as far as the staffing is concerned, it is intended that students from a wide range of opinions should be brought together in order to learn from one another.

If your purpose is to serve overseas with a missionary society it is wise, if at all possible, to make at least an informal approach to a society before you decide where to train. Some, like the Church Missionary Society and Worldwide Evangelisation Crusade have their own college. Many others prefer their candidates to attend particular colleges.

If you are aiming at the home pastoral ministry you will need to take into consideration your own denomination's requirements. For instance if you are an Anglican, a Methodist, or a member of the United Reformed Church you will be required to do a full course at one of the recognised denominational colleges. You may if you wish precede this with a spell at one of the Bible Colleges, but this will not normally be regarded by the denominational authorities as part of your training. The most you can expect is that if you pass a degree or university diploma this will gain you certain exemptions in later college examinations, or pave the way to a second degree or diploma. It will not lessen the requirements of your denomination.

To some extent the Baptist denomination is the same. The candidate for the ministry is expected to attend a Baptist college. However, for those who cannot do this there is another way into the ranks of the ministry by means of what is called the Baptist Union Examination. This is normally done by correspondence while exercising full-time ministry. A Bible College course, if it has led to a University degree or diploma can give exemption from the major part of this examination.

Fees have not been included partly because they vary a great deal – between £200 and £600 per annum – and partly because they frequently have to be changed. Most colleges have bursary schemes, but the first likely source of financial aid will be your Local Education Authority.

ANGLICAN COLLEGES

BISHOP THOMAS BURGESS THEOLOGICAL HALL

Part of St David's University College, Lampeter, Cardiganshire. SA48 7ED. Trains men for the Anglican ministry, and women for the deaconess order.

Courses: Basic courses are the Diploma in Theology (Lampeter) and the certificate in Pastoral Studies;

B.A. Honours in Theology (Wales) for non-graduates;

B.A. or M.A. in Theology (Wales) or Licence in Theology (Lampeter) for graduates.

CHICHESTER THEOLOGICAL COLLEGE

Westgate, Chichester, Sussex.

The College stands within the Catholic tradition of the Church of England. About 50 students can be accommodated, and these may include married men.

Courses: The Certificate in Theology of Southampton University;

General Ordination Examination;

Tuition for external degrees.

CRANMER HALL

Part of St John's College, University of Durham, DH1 3RJ. Evangelical. The 61 students (men and women) of Cranmer Hall are members of the University studying for the ministry, overseas work, and a variety of other Christian callings. The other part of St John's College, St John's Hall is for Christians who probably will not be ordained, but who wish to study some other course as a Christian vocation.

Courses: General Ordination Examination;

Cambridge Certificate in Religious Knowledge;

B.A. Honours in Theology;

Post-graduate degrees, M.A., M.Litt., Ph.D.;

Diploma in Theology;

Diploma in Biblical Studies.

CUDDESDON COLLEGE
Oxford, OX9 9EX.

The College stands in the Catholic tradition of the Church of England. Its stated aim is to be 'devoted to theological enquiry and sets out to explore new methods of training men for the ministry'.

Most students are already graduates of another university.

Courses: Oxford Theological Colleges' Certificate in Theology;
B.A. Oxford;
Diploma in Theology.

EDINBURGH THEOLOGICAL COLLEGE (Scottish Episcopal)
Rosebery Crescent, Edinburgh, EH12 5JT.

One of the oldest Anglican colleges it caters for 26 men students, some of whom are married.

Courses: General Ordination Examination;
Edinburgh University degrees – B.A., M.A., B.D., Licentiate in Theology.

KING'S COLLEGE
The Strand, London, WC2R 2LS.

An integral part of London University, King's has over 200 men and women studying theology as an academic discipline. Those who wish to go on to ordination in the Anglican Church must spend a further year at St Augustine's College, Canterbury, where practical work and further study is undertaken.

Courses: B.A. (London) including theology;
B.D. (London);
A.K.C. (Associate of King's College) which is a recognised ordination qualification, and may be taken with the B.D.;
Higher degrees, M.Th., M.Phil., Ph.D.

LINCOLN THEOLOGICAL COLLEGE
The Bishop's Hostel, Lincoln, LN1 3BP.

Accepts 50 men and 17 women students. Theologically it is

described as 'Liberal Catholic', but has a wide range of Anglican opinion among staff and students.

Courses: General Ordination Examination;
Inter-Diocesan Certificate (women);
B.Th. (Nottingham);
Diploma in Theology (Nottingham) – post-graduate;
Also there are facilities for training for the 'auxiliary' ministry.

OAK HILL
Southgate, London, N14 4PS.
Evangelical. Although primarily a college preparing men for the Anglican ministry, it also includes series of lectures on communications, youth work, teaching, and other specialist activities. Lays most emphasis on Biblical teaching, personal devotion, and pastoral ministry.

Courses: General Ordination Examination;
Diploma in Pastoral Studies (compulsory);
Diploma in Theology (London);
B.D. (London);
M.Th. (London) post-graduate;
S.Th. (Lambeth);
There is a part-time course for those preparing for the 'auxiliary' ministry.

RIDLEY HALL
Cambridge, CB3 9HG.
Seeks to 'combine evangelical principles with careful and open scholarship'. While retaining its evangelical identity the college is entering into a close federation with Westcott House (Anglican) and Wesley House (Methodist).

Courses: General Ordination Examination;
B.A. (Cambridge);
Certificate in Theology (Cambridge) – post-graduate;
Certificate in Pastoral Theology.

107

RIPON HALL
Berkeley Road, Boars Hill, Oxford, OX1 5ES.

As well as Anglican ordinands, other students, both Anglican and from other denominations, are welcomed as an important part of a Theological College's life. It claims to be 'in no sense a party college', and accepts men or women. An integrated syllabus covers theological, pastoral, and sociological studies. The Urban Ministry Project is an important part of the facilities, offering training to ministers, teachers, social, and community workers to enable them to relate the Christian message to the needs of city life.

Courses: General Ordination Examination;

Certificate in Theology;

B.A. (Oxford);

B.D. (London);

A number of other degree and diploma courses are open to graduates.

COLLEGE OF THE RESURRECTION
Mirfield, Yorkshire.

The college is within the Catholic tradition of the Church of England, and has very close links with the Community of the Resurrection in whose grounds it stands. Graduates are preferred.

Courses: General Ordination Examination;

Diploma in Theology (Leeds);

B.A. (Leeds).

ST JOHN'S COLLEGE
Bramcote, Nottingham, NG9 3DS.

Evangelical. Over 100 men and women can be accepted and there are special facilities for married students. The college has its own television studio, and students have opportunities to broadcast on Radio Nottingham. Training methods are being constantly developed and refined to enable Christians to cope with future patterns of ministry.

Courses: B.Th. (Nottingham);

B.A. (Nottingham);

Diploma in Theology (Nottingham);

L.Th. (St John's) – qualifies for Anglican ordination;

Diploma in Pastoral Studies (St John's);

Certificate in Theology (St John's);

Students who are suitably qualified can also be prepared for research degrees. There is a course for the 'auxiliary' ministry.

ST STEPHEN'S HOUSE
Oxford, OX2 6PZ.

Within the Catholic tradition of the Church of England. As well as study there is an emphasis on the development of a disciplined personal spiritual life.

Courses: Oxford Theological Colleges' Certificate in Theology;

B.A. (Oxford);

Diploma in Theology (Oxford);

Post-graduate higher degrees.

SALISBURY AND WELLS
19, The Close, Salisbury, Wilts, SP1 2EE.

Emphasis on liturgical renewal. 'We try to train men using contemporary aids for as wide a form of ministry as is possible.' The college has its own television studio, and has made programmes for both BBC and ITV. Other means of modern communication are studied.

Courses: General Ordination Examination;

Certificate in Theology (Southampton);

Certificate in Theology (Cambridge);

A course is available for preparation for the 'auxiliary' ministry.

TRINITY COLLEGE
Stoke Hill, Bristol, BS9 1JP.

Evangelical. Accepts men and women. Although it is primarily an Anglican college, there is an increasingly interdenominational and international flavour. The college has its own radio studio, and pays particular attention to modern methods of communication.

Courses: B.A. (Bristol);
Diploma in Theology (Bristol);
Certificate of Theology (Bristol);
B.D. (London);
Diploma in Theology (London);
Certificate in Religious Knowledge (London).

WESTCOTT HOUSE
Cambridge.
No details available.

WYCLIFFE HALL
Oxford, 0X2 6PW.
Evangelical. Although primarily an ordination college it accepts an increasing number of graduates who wish to gain a sound training in basic biblical and theological knowledge, together with practical service.

Courses: Pastoralia Certificate (taken by all students);
Certificate in Theology (Oxford);
B.A. (Oxford);
Diploma in Theology (Oxford).

THE QUEEN'S COLLEGE
Somerset Road, Edgbaston, Birmingham, B15 ?QH.
Unlike the above colleges who accept students of other denominations, Queen's is an ecumenical foundation being formed from the original Queen's (Anglican) and Handsworth (Methodist) colleges. Students are not confined to these two denominations.

Courses: General Ordination Examination;
College course;
B.A. (Birmingham);
Diploma in Theology (Birmingham);
Diploma in Pastoral Studies (Birmingham);
Diploma in Liturgy and Church architecture (Birmingham).

Ordination candidates must have been approved by their own denomination.

ORDINATION COURSES

Ordination for ministry within the Anglican Church may, in certain circumstances, be gained by attending one of the part-time courses.

Southwark Ordination Course, St Stephen's Lodge, Hankey Place, SE1.

North West Ordination Course, The Cathedral, Manchester 3.

WILSON CARLILE TRAINING COLLEGE
(Church Army)

27 Vanbrugh Park, Blackheath, SE3 7AG.

Successful students are admitted to the office of Evangelist in the Church by the Archbishop of Canterbury, and are commissioned as Church Army Officers. Theoretical and practical studies cover a wide range of subjects including communication, evangelism, social and moral welfare, children's work, old people. Students, who may be men or women, are normally accepted between the ages of 18 and 35.

BAPTIST COLLEGES

BRISTOL

Woodland Road, Bristol, BS8 1UN.

Men and woman are prepared for the ministry at home and overseas, supplementary ministry, for teaching, for the social services, and other forms of Christian work.

Courses: B.A. (Bristol) – this may be taken in Theology alone or in combination with Philosophy, Sociology, or Politics;

Diploma in Theology (London);

The Certificate of the Bristol Theological Colleges.

IRISH

67 Sandown Road, Belfast, BT5 6GU, Northern Ireland.

'Committed to the truths of the historic evangelical faith.'

Men and women are prepared for the work of the Gospel at home and overseas. The College has special facilities for helping students who have not previously obtained academic qualifications.

Courses: Certificate in Biblical studies;
Theological Diploma;
Diploma in Missionary Studies;
Diploma in Theology (London);
B.D. (London).

NORTHERN

Brighton Grove, Rusholme, Manchester, M14 5JP.
Primarily intended to train students for the Baptist ministry; there is an increasing number of men and women who study Theology without ordination in mind.

Courses: B.A. (Manchester);
Certificate of Theology (Manchester);
B.D. (Manchester) – postgraduate;
Postgraduate Diploma in Social and Pastoral Theology (Manchester).

REGENTS PARK

Oxford.
Permanent private hall of the university, which prepares students (including women) for ordination into the Baptist ministry, but will also accept other students who wish to read an Oxford degree.

Courses: B.A. (Oxford);
Postgraduate studies include Diploma in Theology and the B.Phil., B.Litt., B.D., and D.Phil. degrees.

SPURGEON'S

South Norwood Hill, London, SE25 6DJ.
Men accepted in preparation for the Christian ministry at home and overseas. Normally candidates are expected to have university entrance qualifications, and to pass a preliminary examination in Greek. Preaching experience is also

required. Students not training for the ministry are accepted if space allows.

Courses: B.A. (Council for Academic Awards);
Diploma in Pastoral Studies.

SCOTTISH
31 Oakfield Avenue, Glasgow, GL2 8LL.
Although when space permits private students are accepted to read for a degree, generally speaking the college prepares men for the Baptist ministry or for the Baptist Missionary Society.

Courses: B.A.(Glasgow);
B.D. (London);
Diploma in Theology (London);
College Diploma.

WALES
South Wales Baptist College, 54-58 Richmond Road, Cardiff.
No details available.
Bangor Baptist College, Bangor.
No details available.

METHODIST COLLEGES

BRISTOL
Wesley College, Westbury-on-Trym, Bristol, BS10 7QD.
An affiliated college of Bristol University, and therefore the courses are the same as those listed under Trinity (Anglican) and the Baptist College.

CAMBRIDGE
Wesley House, Jesus Lane, Cambridge, CB5 8BJ.
No details available, but see Ridley Hall (Anglican).

EDGEHILL
Lennoxvale, Belfast, BT9 5BY.
Combines with the two Irish Presbyterian Colleges to train

men and women for the B.D. or Diploma in Theology of the Queen's University of Belfast.

QUEEN'S
See under Anglican.

Note that Methodist training for the ministry or for the Methodist Missionary Society is centrally organised and prospective candidates should write to the Division of Ministries, 1 Central Buildings, London, SW1H 9NH, rather than to an individual college.

CLIFF COLLEGE
Calver, via Sheffield, Yorks, S30 1XG.
A lay training college, Cliff aims to help young people to find their vocation, to get to know their Bible, and to think through their faith. Although a Methodist college, there is no denominational bias in teaching or entry requirements. The basic one-year course provides a sound preparation for further training for social work, overseas and home ministry, youth work, and a variety of other specialised functions. Particular emphasis is laid on studying modern methods of evangelism.

UNITED REFORMED CHURCH

CAMBRIDGE – WESTMINSTER AND CHESHUNT COLLEGES
Madingley Road, Cambridge, CB3 0AA.
Primarily intended for postgraduates, although some older men are accepted. A three-year ordination course is provided as well as advanced degree and research facilities.

LONDON – NEW COLLEGE
527 Finchley Road, Hampstead, NW3 7BE.
The college provides a four-year course for ordination

candidates as well as catering for those who intend to specialise in Religious Education.

Courses: B.D. (London);
  M.Th., M.Phil., Ph.D. (London);
  Diploma in Theology (London) – ministerial students only.

MANCHESTER – THE CONGREGATIONAL COLLEGE

Whalley Range, Manchester, M16 8BP.
Courses are similar to those offered by the Northern Baptist College.

OXFORD – MANSFIELD COLLEGE

Oxford, OX1 3TA.
This is a constituent part of the university and therefore all students must be qualified to take a university degree or diploma. Because of its situation, the college tends to produce a high proportion of theological teachers. All denominations are accepted.

Courses: B.A. Honours (Oxford);
  A variety of higher degrees and diplomas, including B.Litt., D.Phil., B.D., B.C.L.

SWANSEA – MEMORIAL COLLEGE

Ffynhonnau, Swansea.
A college that has a distinguished history stretching right back to the Puritans. Ordinands of any denomination are accepted, and also other students who wish to study theology.

Courses: B.D. (Wales);
  Diploma in Theology (Wales);
  Diploma in Pastoral Theology (Wales);
  College ministerial certificate.

OTHER THEOLOGICAL COLLEGES

ST COLM'S COLLEGE
23 and 24 Inverleith Terrace, Edinburgh, EH3 5NX.
A residential college of the Church of Scotland which trains men and women for home and overseas mission and deaconess work.
Courses: A two-year course for intending home missionaries;

A one-year course mainly for those who already have obtained a professional qualification and who wish to go overseas.

FREE CHURCH OF SCOTLAND COLLEGE
The Mound, Edinburgh, EH1 2LS.
The college stands for 'loyalty to the inspired Word of God ... and acceptance of the Westminster Confession of Faith.' It is a non-residential course, and candidates for the ministry are expected to have previously secured a first degree.
Courses: B.D. (Edinburgh);

College Diploma.

BRITISH ISLES NAZARENE COLLEGE
Dene Road, Didsbury, Manchester, M20 8GU.
The college is based on the theology of the Holiness Movement and is open to men or women. It takes the view that all Christian young people ought to be at their best academically, and therefore courses are open to non-ordinands.
Courses: B.Th.;

College Diploma;

Churchmanship Certificate.

PRESBYTERIAN COLLEGE
Botanic Avenue, Belfast, BT7 1JT.
A combined college with Magee (Presbyterian) Theological College, and Edgehill (Methodist). The staff are recognised by Queen's University, Belfast, as the teaching members of the Faculty of Theology.

Courses: B.D. (Belfast);
Diploma in Theology (Belfast);
Certificate in Biblical Studies;
Higher degrees – M.Th., Ph.D., D.D.

THE SELLY OAK COLLEGES
Birmingham, B29 6LE.
This is a federation of autonomous colleges, and includes non-theological ones. A wide variety of courses and recreational and creative facilities are offered centrally.

1. WOODBROOKE
Society of Friends. Provides preparation for various forms of Christian service. A special feature includes the study of the principles and practice of the Society of Friends.

2. KINGSMEAD
Sponsored by the Methodist Missionary Society. Students are prepared for missionary and social work.

3. WESTHILL
A voluntary College of Education. As well as offering training for teachers, courses are also provided for youth and community service, and Church education.

4. OVERDALE
Churches of Christ. Provides a four-year course for ordinands, which may include a degree. Also there are short courses for lay workers.

5. COLLEGE OF THE ASCENSION
United Society for Propagating the Gospel. Training for missionaries.

6. ST ANDREWS HALL
For missionary candidates for the Baptist Missionary Society, the Congregational Council for World Mission, and The Presbyterian Church.

7. CROWTHER HALL
Missionary candidates for the Church Missionary Society.

SALVATION ARMY
International Training College, Denmark Hill, London, SE5 8BQ.

The Salvation Army officer may engage in a wide variety of types of Christian service – local pastoral and evangelistic work, specialised service in approved schools, prisons, hostels, hospitals, among children and the elderly are just some of them. Excellent literature is available which gives a clear picture of the openings and the requirements. Training lasts five years – one year pre-college, two years at the International Training College, and two years post-college.

The following colleges come under the broad classification of non-denominational Bible or Missionary Training Colleges. Without exception they are specifically evangelical in theology.

ALL NATIONS' CHRISTIAN COLLEGE
Easneye, Ware, Herts, SG12 8LX.

A combination of the All Nations' Missionary College, and the women's training colleges, Mount Hermon and Ridgelands. The aim of the college is to equip students for worldwide ministry. There is an emphasis on modern methods of communicating the Gospel. All candidates are expected to have some professional or vocational training.

Courses: The basic course is a two-year College Diploma, but the emphasis is on tailor-made courses to suit individuals;

Refresher courses for missionaries;

Diploma in Theology (London).

ASSEMBLIES OF GOD BIBLE COLLEGE
Mattersey Hall, Mattersey, Doncaster, Yorks, DN10 5HD.

As well as aiming to equip young men and women for Christian service there is a strong emphasis on spiritual development, with special courses on Pentecostal teaching on the Holy Spirit. Journalism, radio technique, and public relations are among the 'extras' taught.

Courses: College Diploma (two years);

Special short courses;

Correspondence courses.

BELFAST BIBLE COLLEGE

119 Marlborough Park South, Belfast, BT9 6HW.

The basis for the courses for men and women is a thorough exegesis of the whole Bible. Students are prepared for a wide variety of service at home and overseas.

Courses: College Diploma;
College Certificate;
Certificate of Religious Knowledge (London);
Diploma in Theology (London);
Evening classes.

BIBLE TRAINING INSTITUTE

64 Bothwell Street, Glasgow, G2 7JB, Scotland.

No details available.

BIRMINGHAM BIBLE INSTITUTE

6 Pakenham Road, Edgbaston, Birmingham 15.

No details available.

CHELSTON BIBLE COLLEGE

Spencer Road, New Milton, Hants, BH25 5JB.

Exists specifically to provide intensive short courses (of one–three terms) for Christians who as yet have no definite calling, nor three years to give to a normal college course. Improvement in knowledge of the Bible and its use in Christian service is the aim.

BIBLE COLLEGE OF WALES

Derwen Fawr, Swansea, SA2 8EB.

The college provides a two-year course for men or women, and is concerned primarily with preparation for overseas missionary work.

CAPERNWRAY HALL

Near Carnforth, Lancs.

The intention is to provide short intensive courses of Bible study and related subjects to enable students to return to their normal occupations better equipped to serve and witness. In fact many go on to further training and then into some form of full-time ministry.

Courses: School Certificate, or a variety of intensive courses, lasting from eight to 30 weeks;
Correspondence courses.

ELIM BIBLE COLLEGE
Capel, Surrey.

Although Pentecostal, men and women students from other denominations are welcome. A balanced course is provided, and special facilities include training for the ministry of music, a recording studio, and a college drama group.

Courses: College Diploma – two years;
Certificate of Religious Knowledge (London);
Diploma in Theology (London);
Correspondence courses.

EMMANUEL BIBLE COLLEGE
1 Palm Grove, Birkenhead, L43 1TE.

The college aims to give its students a sound Biblical knowledge with special emphasis on 'full salvation'. Preparation is given for all types of Christian service.

Courses: College Missionary Diploma;
College Ministerial Diploma;
Certificate of Religious Knowledge (London);
Diploma in Theology (London).

FAITH MISSION BIBLE COLLEGE
18 Ravelston Park, Edinburgh, EH4 3DZ.

The primary aim of the college is to prepare young men and women for work with the Faith Mission. The two-year course emphasises Bible teaching and character training.

HILDENBOROUGH HALL
Otford Hills, Sevenoaks, Kent, TN15 6XL.

As well as regular conferences, Hildenborough runs an eight-month course of residential studies for young people.

It is designed for those who wish to gain a comprehensive understanding of basic Christian beliefs and behaviour.

KENSIT MEMORIAL BIBLE COLLEGE
104 Hendon Lane, Finchley, N3 3SQ.
A small college originally founded to train Wickliffe Preachers for the Protestant Truth Society. Now the college is open to all – men or women – and prepares students for all kinds of pastoral and missionary work.
Courses: The basic college course of three years;
    Certificate of Religious Knowledge (London);
    Diploma in Theology (London);
    B.D. (London);
    Special one-term short course.

LEBANON MISSIONARY BIBLE COLLEGE
Castle Terrace, Berwick-on-Tweed, Northumberland TD15 1PA.
Aims to provide intellectual and spiritual training for those wishing to meet the modern missionary challenge.
Courses: Diploma of Proficiency in Biblical, Theological
    and Missionary studies;
    Diploma of Missionary Training;
    Special short courses;
    Correspondence courses.

LONDON BIBLE COLLEGE
Green Lane, Northwood, Middlesex, HA6 2UW.
Designed to give men and women a thoroughly scholarly and practical knowledge of the Christian faith, and to prepare them for various forms of service.
Courses: B.A. (Council of National Academic Awards);
    Diploma in Theology (London);
    Advanced degrees – M.Th., Ph.D.;
    Correspondence and evening courses.

MOORLANDS BIBLE COLLEGE
Sopley Park, Christchurch, Hampshire.

Offers a balanced curriculum that is theological, spiritual, evangelical, and practical.

Courses: College Diploma – two years;
College Associateship – three years;
Diploma in Theology (London);
Special short courses.

REDCLIFFE MISSIONARY TRAINING COLLEGE
66 Grove Park Road, Chiswick, London W4.
Trains women primarily for overseas missionary work. Students must already have experience in a job or profession suitable for missionary work.
Courses: Two-year Proficiency Diploma.

ROMSEY HOUSE
274 Mill Road, Cambridge, CB1 3NQ.
A wide variety of subjects is covered to help men and women in their preparation for Christian service at home and overseas.
Courses: B.D. (London);
Diploma in Theology (Cambridge);
Diploma in Theology (London);
Certificate of Theology (Cambridge);
Missionary Training Course;
Romsey House Diploma.

SOUTH WALES BIBLE COLLEGE
Weston Square, Barry, Glamorgan, CF6 7YD.
Training is provided for men and women, for home and overseas work. The main emphasis is on Biblical exegesis and Christian doctrine. Reformation theology provides the basis of the college's teaching. Courses are either two or three years for the College Diploma.

WORLDWIDE EVANGELISATION CRUSADE MISSIONARY TRAINING COLLEGE
10 Prince Albert Road, Glasgow, G12 9NW.
Primarily designed for candidates for overseas work with

W.E.C. or its sister society, Christian Literature Crusade. Others who are not yet clear as to their future service may be accepted, and special arrangements are sometimes made to train the approved candidates of other societies.

Courses: College Certificate – two years;
Certificate of Religious Knowledge (London).

The above notes are inevitably sketchy and do scant justice to the enormous amount of thought, planning, and in some cases imagination which has gone into the courses. You should write to any colleges that seem to be offering the kind of training you want. In most cases you will receive a prompt and helpful reply with literature that will give you a much more vivid and complete picture than is possible here. If possible visit the college you choose before you apply.

In the case of a denominational college, since you must gain the approval of your denomination before you proceed to training, there is little point in writing to colleges at the outset.

As you will have noticed, many of the colleges listed here offer tuition for degrees and university diplomas. If you wish to follow such a course you will need to fulfil the normal university entrance requirements. You would be well advised to write to the university concerned to discover what those requirements are.

Frequently it is difficult to draw distinctions between colleges, and so the classification adopted here is only to be understood broadly. In addition it should be noted that a number of universities have faculties of theology, which, although not strictly theological colleges, do prepare students for ordination and other forms of Christian service. This is true, for instance, at Edinburgh, Glasgow, St Andrews, Aberdeen and Belfast.

What can you expect?

Success or failure? Which is it to be? Is it right to talk about it anyway?

Basically there are two opposing and mutually exclusive views on the subject. There are Christians who believe that outward signs of success are inevitably signs of God's favour. Because I've done well in business, it shows that God approves of me. Because I'm the minister of a big Church it must mean that God is pleased with my ministry. Because I'm in charge of directing this big organisation, God must be more than satisfied with my performance.

But such a view is both unscriptural and ludicrous. If it were true then its opposite would be equally so – the poor man, the minister of a run-down Church, the humble clerk in a big organisation – all these would presumably be under God's disfavour.

The Old Testament writers had to face the same problem. They saw a wealthy man like Abraham, and they assumed that his success was to be traced to the fact that he was the 'friend of God'. But then they saw that other men, who were far from being God's friends, were wealthy too. They had to learn that there is no necessary connection between God's favour and a man's success. As the Psalmist puts it 'It is better to have little and be godly than to own an evil man's wealth' (Ps. 37:16).

A quite opposite view is held by those who regard success as a dirty word. They point out that the word doesn't occur in the Bible, and therefore it shouldn't enter into the calculations of the Christian. 'What God expects,' they say, 'is faithfulness, not success.' If this is the whole truth, then the young person who leaves college with high hopes has only himself to blame if that early optimism is dispersed by frustration and failure.

The trouble springs from our misunderstanding of what success is. Almost always it is linked in our minds with money, or fame, or status. In other words, we define it in terms of external factors which we can easily measure. When the Church offerings go up or crowds flock to a meeting we call it success because that is something tangible, and we can quantify it.

If this were a true view of success, then we would need to write off the ministry of Christ as a failure. How else can you regard the facts? He began well enough, with the crowds hanging enthusiastically on his every word. Then things went sour. The crowds began to dwindle. Opposition grew. Finally he died a criminal's death.

To be accurate, we should define success as the achievement of one's aims. Immediately it is evident that in this sense Jesus was a tremendous success. Had he intended to gather a large organisation around himself, or wanted to overthrow the system and set up a new popular religious party, then maybe the lone figure on the cross was a failure. But in fact his aim was very different. His intention was to provide the means of salvation that you and I need. In that he was wholly successful.

In this sense it is plain that the New Testament regards success as a perfectly proper thing for the Christian to expect and work for. The story of the sower in Luke 8 underlines this. The sower expects the seed to work – otherwise he wouldn't bother to sow it. He sets out with a clear aim, and the harvest he achieves is a measure of his success.

Frequently our failures in Christian work can be traced to the lack of a clear goal. Instead of getting it clear in our minds what we are after, we have a vague, general idea. We aim, for instance, at 'God's blessing', which can then be interpreted in almost any way we choose.

One minister I know begins each year by deciding on a few carefully chosen objectives, and then he goes all out on them. It is surprising how often at the end of the year those objectives are achieved.

Many of us fail to achieve the success he enjoys because we have not taken the trouble to sit down and define our aims. As a result we spread our efforts too wide. We see so many needs crying out to be met, but trying to meet them all results in effort being dissipated and success being small. At the end of a year of hard work we see little return for our strenuous efforts and we are ripe for discouragement.

Mark you, there are other factors involved, as the story of the sower makes clear. For instance, it is a story about growth. Usually growth, to be worthwhile, is steady and undramatic. This is a problem for us. We like instant success. Sometimes we even fall to the temptation of trying to create artificial results. We pressurise people, we manipulate events, we gloss over failures, simply in order to justify ourselves with immediate success. But success should be seen in terms of growth. Lasting results may not be evident for months or even years.

Further, the parable is by no means an unbroken success story. Three out of the four different types of soil were unfruitful. Not that we should therefore deduce that three-quarters of our work will fail, but we should be realistic. We are generally afraid of admitting failure. At the end of an evangelistic crusade, for instance, we sometimes hear it said 'There were no conversions, but the Church was richly blessed'. Assuming that the aim of such a crusade is to bring about conversions, then it has apparently failed. Why not say so? Or at least admit that we hadn't clarified our aims sufficiently in the first place? The New Testament is much more honest than we are. It tells us when Paul's preaching produced hundreds of converts. It also tells us when it cut no ice at all.

But still we haven't quite come to the heart of the matter. To define success as 'the achievement of one's aims' is only part of the truth. For the Christian, success needs to be described as 'the achievement of *Christ's* aims'. And unfor-

126

tunately his aims and ours do not always coincide. We may indeed achieve our objectives, but our success will be hollow if Christ had another purpose in mind.

It is important to grasp this principle and to live by it, for it will not only remove many of the inner tensions and frustrations that lead to discouragement, it will also prevent us from judging our own results and those of other people by the wrong standards.

Remember the young man at the beginning of chapter one? He said he felt called to the ministry, but what followed? I doubt very much if he could be called a success in the sense that he achieved his aims, for I'm sure his aims did not include one brief, tough pastorate after another. Nor, I am certain, could he be described as a success by the standards of measurement we normally adopt – no great congregation flocking to hear his preaching, no flood of invitations to speak at this rally or that convention, no fashionable Church begging him to become their minister, no denominational honours. So? He's a failure isn't he?

In his case, I doubt it. There have been conversions through his preaching – not many, but some. Several of the Churches where he worked were in a terrible state with quarrels, discouragement, unspirituality and worldliness as their hallmarks. He has left them stronger and straighter for someone else to come and make a 'success' of them. People have spoken of the immense comfort and strength he has been when they have been ill or in a time of personal crisis. You can't call that failure. Maybe he could have been more successful, but if Christ's aims for those Churches and individuals were being achieved, it was success.

So whatever the specialised function you undertake, don't be guided by the outward success that can be measured – although you can thank God for it if it comes.

Don't be over-concerned with what other people think you should do or achieve.

Your responsibility is to discover and carry out Christ's

aims for you. Then you will be absolutely certain of total success.

*   *   *

A prayer:

Teach us, good Lord, to serve thee as thou deservest; to give and not to count the cost; to fight and not to heed the wounds; to toil and not to seek for rest; to labour and not to ask for any reward, save that of knowing that we do Thy will; through Jesus Christ our Lord.

AMEN.